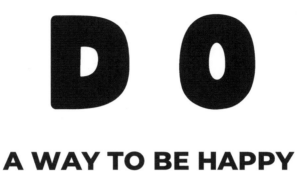

DO

**A WAY TO BE HAPPY
ALL THE TIME**

HAPPY

GIHAN 'DR G' JAYAWEERA

First published in 2024 by Hambone Publishing
www.hambonepublishing.com.au

 A catalogue record for this book is available from the National Library of Australia

Editing by Mish Phillips, Lexi Wight and Sadie Butterworth-Jones

Book design and layout: Sadie Butterworth-Jones
www.luneviewpublishing.co.uk

For information about this title, contact:
Gihan Jayaweera | drg@drgihan.com | www.drgihan.com

Paperback ISBN 978-1-922357-78-6
eBook ISBN 978-1-922357-79-3

To my parents, my wife and the person I was.

Foreword

The first time I heard about 'G', I was heading to an event at Adelaide University. "You should see this guy dance, he is amazing!" The legends were true, the boy could indeed move. Several years later I was heading to a social cricket game. "They have this one guy named G; he will be the best player there." Who was this cricket bat-wielding, hip hop-dancing legend?

Fast forward many years later to a global pandemic, when a family walk around my new neighbourhood led to a chance encounter with the man now known as 'Dr G'. Even amongst a once-in-a-generation pandemic there can be some glimmers of hope, this fortuitous meeting was one of them. Interestingly, in those first few weeks of our budding friendship, I don't recall talking about our mutual love of cricket or hip hop. Instead, I distinctly remember, on our first jog together, hypothesising what happens to us after death (we obviously chose to skip the small talk).

It seemed like we were both going through transition periods in our lives and more often than not we would end up trying to dissect that weighty topic of happiness. We didn't always take the same approach but overwhelmingly agreed on the importance of our most basic human needs of social connection, physical activity, nutrition, and sleep. Over the past few years, our mutual respect for each other has continued to flourish and I always come away from our conversations with something new to ponder.

Dr G's book will give readers practical advice that will help steer you towards happiness, and I can most certainly vouch that he is someone who practises what he preaches. Whether you are looking for modern-day implications for the ancient wisdom of Eastern philosophy, or practical advice for the busy individual, this book will have something for everyone. His writing is always insightful and honest, as is the man himself. His genuine desire to help the wellbeing of others permeates throughout his work and even more so when you meet him, which I believe is his greatest strength.

From the multi-talented myth that was G, to my knowledgeable new friend that was Dr. G, I now just know him as Gihan. He is a dear friend and my spiritual partner in crime. I am incredibly proud of what he has achieved, and am truly honoured to make this small contribution to his work.

Much love to you all.

Mahesh "Heshy P" Paramasivan

Contents

Introduction

Why I wrote this book

Life slaps everyone in the face. The first time *I* was slapped was in high school. I had big ears, a receding hairline and a massive afro. To any seasoned bully, I looked like lunch. I was teased. A lot. There were a lot of tears during this period. Just to be clear, I wasn't bullied for the afro. The afro was epic.

In high school, I had a singular focus: get into medical school. I worked my ass off. By the time I finished high school, I had no ass. I thought that if I worked hard and made enough sacrifices, things would be easier in university. Medical school was harder than high school.

Time for another big slap.

I was only 17 years old when I entered medical school. I grew up in Melbourne so studying in Adelaide meant that I spent most of the year away from my family, my closest friends and my girlfriend, who I now call my wife — don't worry, she knows I call her that. It is true what they say about medical school. It is demanding. In the first week, we had to learn all about the heart. By the second week, I was already behind. I was also surrounded by geniuses, which welcomed years of self-doubt and questions about whether I was good enough.

Medical school was also the season of being broke. Not the kind of broke that had me worrying about where my next meal would come from, but the kind where my girlfriend had to buy my phone credit so that we could maintain our long-distance relationship. It was embarrassing but I stubbornly refused to get a job in university. I thought work experience was for people who didn't want to lie on their resume. My assumption was that I could pay for my own phone credit when I was a doctor. I was right.

It all came to a head during my 5th year of medical school. This is the "barrier year". We were tested on all of our five years of coursework. If you failed even one exam, you had to repeat the whole year. Pressure makes diamonds, right? For me, pressure made anxiety. I couldn't control the result of the exam, so I started to control other areas of my life. Things got weird. I used to tighten the taps and then run my hand under the tap to see if there was any water still coming out. If my hand felt even a drop of water, I would go back to tightening the tap and the cycle would start again. I would go to bed and wonder, "Did I close the tap?" I had a similar relationship with locks on doors and burners on stoves. I would quadruple-check that the front door or the car door was properly locked, and that the stove was off. I was never fully confident, "What if the door was open?" or "What if the gas is still on?" that intrusive voice would ask me.

When I tell this story now, I realise how ridiculous this sounds. At the time, I would have told you that I was "stressed". It never struck me as abnormal. Medical students were only supposed to learn about illnesses. We were not supposed to get them.

Fast forward to 2013. I collapsed in a heap at the foot of my bed. I had just received my grades for my final year of medical school. I passed. But at what cost? For the last five years, I had sacrificed my happiness and health so I could pass my exams. My diet had been all over the place. I ate at odd times and sometimes not at all. I went to sleep late and woke up early after pressing snooze for the seventh time. The only consistent exercise I got was running to class because I was always late. I had great friends but the stress prevented me from being fully present. My life was busy. My mind was busier. In that moment, curled at the foot of my bed, I vowed to myself:

"I am never going to let this happen to me again.
It is not worth it. It is never worth it."

Medical school almost broke me, but without all of this suffering, you wouldn't be reading this book. Studying interstate was difficult but it had a hidden blessing: the airport bookshop. While I waited for my flights, I looked through any book I could find on happiness, wellbeing, and personal development. I had a life-changing realisation. *For every problem that I faced in my life, someone had written a book about it.*

I had a problem: I was unhappy. I knew I just needed to find the right books. I became good at reading (i.e. gaining knowledge) and then implementing it (i.e. applying that knowledge). Knowing and not doing is not knowing, so I ensured that I had a heavy bias towards *action*. It felt like a science experiment. I was constantly experimenting with different strategies. Some worked, some didn't, but I always learned.

When Thomas Edison was working on inventing the light bulb he made 1,000 unsuccessful attempts. He said, "I didn't fail 1,000 times. The light bulb was an invention with 1,000 steps." Thankfully, becoming happy didn't require that many steps.

After years of trial and error I discovered the insight that changed my life. *Happiness is a skill.* Like any skill, it can be learnt. Like anything that can be learnt, it can be taught. It is the skill of happiness that I will unpack in this book.

The statistics

The mental health statistics in Australia are shocking.

As of 2024, the latest research by the Australian Bureau of Statistics (ABS) and the Australian Institute of Health and Welfare (AIHW) showed:
- Approximately 9 Australians take their own life every day.
- Over 2 in 5 Australians (8.5 million people) between the age of 16 and 85 have experienced a mental health disorder in their lifetime.
- Over 1 in 5 Australians (4.3 million people) between the age of 16 and 85 had a mental disorder that lasted at least 12 months.

- Nearly 2 in 5 young Australians aged between 16 and 24 (700,000 people) have experienced a mental health disorder in the last 12 months.
- 1 in 7 children and adolescents (628,000 people) aged between 4 and 17 experienced a mental illness.
- 65% of adolescents don't seek help for mental illness.
- 18% of the Australian population (4.8 million people) have filled a mental health related prescription.

These numbers are *unacceptable*.

The mental health epidemic is one of the biggest social problems we face. Given such staggering statistics, at least one of the following will be true:
1. You will be affected.
2. Someone you care about will be affected.

Even if you tried, you cannot ignore it.

My work as a doctor puts me in a unique position. When I see these statistics, I don't see numbers, I see *real* people:
» The 11-year-old boy in primary school who is getting bullied and anxious about going to school.
» The 21-year-old girl who is depressed and suicidal after going through a break up.
» The 34-year-old husband and father of two who is overwhelmed with trying to balance work, marriage, and life.
» The 41-year-old mother who put her children first for years and lost touch with herself in the process.

» The 52-year-old man who after 20 years of marriage is getting divorced and needs to drink wine every night just to calm his nerves and sleep.

» The 74-year-old woman who is crumbling under the stress of caring for her husband with dementia and the guilt of moving him to a nursing home, which she knows he will hate.

» The 94-year-old woman in the nursing home who is depressed and lonely about her loss of independence and purpose.

For every individual that is affected, there is a ripple effect that extends to family, friends, and colleagues. To paraphrase the late English poet John Donne, "No person is an island." The interconnectedness of our lives means that if one of us suffers, we all suffer.

Once, I was in a consult with a young girl who was suicidal. She had booked a 15-minute appointment. It took 65 minutes. We shared a heavy conversation. I try to not let this stuff affect me, but in this instance, it did. After she left, the next patient was visibly angry with me for "making him wait for so long." I was already a bit shaken by the previous consult so I said something I instantly regretted, "What's with the attitude?"

The patient stood up, pointed at me, and told me that "I shouldn't be sitting in that seat." He stormed out of the room and complained to the receptionist. The receptionist was left shaken and surprised by the encounter.

The receptionist's suffering stemmed from the young girl who she didn't say a single word to.

If one of us suffers, we all suffer.

Throw money at it

I want to commend the efforts that have been taken to combat the mental health epidemic.

According to the Australian Institute of Health and Welfare:
- Spending on mental health related services increased from $10.9 billion in 2017-2018 to $12.2 billion (7% of the total government expenditure) in 2021-22.
- Almost $1.5 billion was spent on mental health related Medicare services (a tiny fraction of this would have been with handsome doctors like me!).
- $672 million was spent on mental health related prescriptions in 2022-23.
- $7.4 billion was spent on state and territory mental health services in 2021-22.

Given these numbers, there is a very important question to ask:

Why are things getting worse?

If you are privileged enough to be reading this book, I assume that you have most, if not all, of your basic needs of food, shelter, water, and safety already met. Australia consistently ranks within the top 10 countries worldwide for its extraordinary standard of living. My measure for standard of living is simple: if you are able to order food through an app on your phone and have a stranger that you don't even have to interact with deliver the food to your doorstep within 30 minutes, you are amongst one of the most privileged human beings in the history of time.

Despite all of this, the mental health of our society is getting worse. *Why?*

Can you be happy *all the time?*

> Charles was an 85-year-old resident in the nursing home where I worked. He was a legend. He devoted his final months to one passion: puzzles. He would spend hours in the library working on them. One day, he decided to take on a 1,000-piece puzzle of the sky, where every piece was a shade of blue or white. Some people just love to suffer. Like any seasoned puzzle master, he started with the borders, grouped similar pieces, and gradually, the sky started to take shape. But as he neared the end, he was shattered: the final piece was missing.

The mental health epidemic is a lot like Charles' puzzle. We're missing pieces, but unlike Charles, we don't always recognize the gaps.

» There is no shortage of mental health awareness campaigns.
» There is no shortage of mental health organisations.
» There is no shortage of tips, tricks, and techniques to improve our mental health.

So why are things still getting worse?

Are we missing the right puzzle pieces?

Let's go a step further.

Are we assembling the wrong puzzle?

The current puzzle focuses on improving mental health. This book, however, is about a different puzzle: one that looks to find a way to be happy *all the time*. Now that's a puzzle worth doing!

I believe that "Good questions will give good answers. Great questions will change your life."

This book tackles the question, "How can I be happy *all the time*?"

As you read that, you likely scoffed at the idea. It's normal to treat me with the same level of suspicion as a late-night infomercial promising 6-pack abs. At first glance, it is a ridiculous proposition. It challenges everything we know about happiness. Good. That's the point.

Do you think it is possible to be happy all the time?

"Whether you think you can,
or you think you can't, you're right."
~ Henry Ford

If you believe it's impossible, you're right. However, you may be reinforcing your own limitations.

But if you believe it's possible, you're right as well. We can now start reverse engineering what would be required to make it a reality.

"The greater danger for most of us is not that our aim is too
high and we miss it. But that it is too low... and we reach it."
~ Michelangelo

I cannot think of aiming higher than being happy all the time.

This is an audacious conversation. I have spent nearly two decades solving the happiness puzzle in my life and now help others do the same. The principles in this book are drawn from my own personal and professional experiences and are grounded in evidence-based methodologies from cognitive behaviour therapy (CBT), positive psychology, acceptance and commitment therapy (ACT), mindfulness, and neuro-linguistic programming (NLP). Every concept within these covers has been extensively tried and tested on myself as well as on my patients and clients. This is not a book about theoretical concepts. It is a call for you, the reader, to learn these principles and *act*. The concepts in this book won't work unless you do. My friend, the book is called *Do Happy* for a reason.

Getting to the root

As a doctor, my passion is to identify and directly address the *root cause* of one's suffering. If someone has a heart attack, they will leave the hospital with a stent in their heart, at least 5 medications, and a new friend they affectionately refer to as "my cardiologist". The cause of this heart attack may be a poor diet, lack of exercise, and smoking. The root cause may be a busy and stressful life that leaves no time and energy left to focus on health.

If someone presents to their doctor with anxiety and depression, the cause may be the loss of a loved one, sickness, a relationship breakdown, or bullying at work. The root cause may be a poor commitment to the fundamentals (Part 2 of this book), an ineffective framework for dealing with uncomfortable and unpleasant emotions (Part 3 of this book), or misunderstanding the nature of life (Part 4 of this book).

This book looks at the root cause: You.

This can be confronting. That is not my intention.

This is one of the crucial pieces of the happiness puzzle. Happiness starts and ends with *you*. If *you* are the reason for your unhappiness, then *you* can be the reason for your happiness. This means that your mental health is not at the whim of the circumstances of your life. It won't rely on how others treat you. It won't be dependent on what happens to you. It will rely solely on your ability to take *full personal ownership of your mental health*. You can learn how to do this. It is a skill.

I hope the prospect of this is not confronting but rather, empowering and liberating.

My wish is that regardless of what happens to you, you can still find a way to be happy. Deal?

Who is this book for?

If you want to become happier, you will love this book.

If you are feeling anxious, depressed, stressed, worried, sad, overwhelmed, or stuck, the mindsets and strategies in this book can dramatically improve your life.

If you have a mental health care plan and you are waiting to see a psychologist, read this book while you wait. Start *acting* on what you learn. Remember, the book is not called "Read Happy".

If you are in need of help but you aren't ready to ask for it (P.S. that's okay, but you should totally ask for help anyway!), let this book be your virtual health professional while you wait for the right time (P.S. the right time was yesterday!).

If you are a leader, you will understand that people are the lifeblood of any organisation. With over 40% of Australian adults experiencing a mental health condition during their lives, it is likely that someone in your team is struggling. I hope this book helps you support them.

If you are a fellow GP/health professional, thank you for your front-line efforts against the mental health crisis. This book will help you improve your own mental health (because we are human too) and better help your patients. It overcomes two common constraints: lack of knowledge and lack of time. Along with a comprehensive understanding of everything you need to know, each chapter is designed to allow focused consultations, where you and your patients can progress step-by-step through the book together.

If you are a psychologist, I hope this book helps you (because you are human too) and serves as a valuable resource that you can recommend to your patients. Thank you for the meaningful work you do.

Who is this book not for?

Although this book would be useful for all readers, it is not tailored for individuals with more complex mental health issues such as trauma, personality disorders, bipolar affective disorder, eating disorders, or psychosis. These conditions often require specialist psychologist and psychiatrist involvement. This book is also not specifically tailored for children. However, as a parent, you can use this information to develop happy habits and lifestyle choices for your family. By modelling these behaviours, you can teach your children how to Do Happy, which is a powerful way for them to learn without being formally taught.

A word about antidepressants

"Half of my friends are on antidepressants."
~ A patient of mine

Mental health related prescriptions are on the rise. In 2019, more than 17% of women and 10% of men were using antidepressants. The Australian Government invested $635 million on mental health related prescriptions between 2021-22. Most people are hesitant to take an antidepressant. There is nothing wrong with being on an antidepressant. For some people, they are life-changing. They are also heavily over-prescribed. There are many people I have met on antidepressants who have not tried or heard of any of the strategies in this book. I am not advocating against antidepressants. This is *not* a book about getting off your antidepressants. It is a book about *personal responsibility* — it's about everything within *your* power that you can do to drastically improve your mental health. If you are on antidepressants and you want to get off them, you must always consult first with your doctor.

There is nothing wrong with you. Ever.

Over the years, I have met a lot of people who are anxious, depressed, sad, worried, stressed, overwhelmed, and burnt out. An even greater proportion of people are "meh", where things are okay but there is a nagging scnsc that it could be better. These experiences can often lead people to believe that there is something inherently wrong with them.

"Everyone else seems to have it all together, why don't I? There must be something wrong with me. Perhaps I am deficient in some way."

Picture me getting on top of a table, clearing my throat and saying the following:

"There is nothing wrong with you. Ever."

You may just need to do a few things differently. If you think that something is wrong with you, I sincerely thank you for the opportunity to prove you wrong.

How to read and use this book

This book is called **Do Happy** for a reason. If you want your life to get better, there is only one thing you can rely on: *action*. Action is the only thing that will create results in your life. In the *Do Happy* framework, there are 3 P's of action: Physical, Psychological, and Perspectival.

Physical action relates to what we physically do.
Psychological action relates to changing our thinking patterns.
Perspectival action relates to shifting our perspective, our mindset, and how we see the world, to understand the nature of the world and our minds.

I hope you take the time to read the book cover to cover. Each chapter explores important principles and actions that you can take towards your own happiness. However, more than reading the book, my wish is that you prioritise action. I would rather you read one chapter and apply its strategy than read the entire book and implement nothing.

Read *actively*: underline, highlight, write notes in the margins, and dog-ear the pages. Reading should be a contact sport! This book is for *you*, so use it in the way that benefits you the most.

Book breakdown

Part 1: The Theory introduces the concept of "Doing Happy" and helps you become familiar with the three words you need to understand to master your mental health: feelings, thoughts, and actions.

Part 2: The Fundamental Skills — Physical Action outlines the nine fundamental physical actions for achieving greater happiness: Exercise, Sleep, Nutrition, Relationships, Nature, Kindness, Gratitude, Meditation for Focus and Replacing Screens. When I see someone who is struggling with their mental health, it is often due to a lack of commitment to these fundamentals. If all we do is commit to these fundamental actions, my belief is that the mental health epidemic would be no more. These actions are common sense but not common practice. I hope this book changes that.

Part 3: The Intermediate Skills — Psychological Action focuses on changing our thinking to become happier. As Marcus Aurelius once said, *"The happiness of your life depends upon the quality of your thoughts"*.

Mastering our inner world, particularly our thoughts, will transform our life in ways that are beyond imagination.

Part 4: The Advanced Skills — Perspectival Action delves into reshaping our perspectives on how we perceive the world, ourselves and happiness itself. While committing to the physical and psychological actions of Doing Happy can lead to extraordinary happiness, perspectival action can help us experience a form of happiness that carries deep wisdom and requires no conditions. These shifts in perspective will help you grasp what it truly means to be happy *all the time*.

Each chapter has a "Dr G's prescription", that invites you to act. Here is the first one:

Dr G's prescription

To help you commit to action, I have designed a free downloadable workbook that accompanies this book. Download it here — <u>drgihan. com/dohappyworkbook</u>. To get the most out of this book, print the workbook and fill it out as you go.

Privacy and confidentiality

I learn a lot from my patients and clients and therefore this book shares a lot of their stories. Unless I have explicitly gained permission to use their name, all examples in this book have been de-identified to protect their privacy. They have been anonymized to such an extent that even they themselves would probably not recognise their own story.

Let's pull the arrow out

In one of his analogies, the Dalai Lama contrasts the Western and Eastern approaches to dealing with suffering using the metaphor of being shot by an arrow. He explains that the Western approach to psychology traditionally delves into questions of why the arrow was shot, how it was shot, and who shot it. The emphasis is on making sense of what has *already* happened to you in the past. The Eastern approach focuses on *pulling the arrow out*. Instead of asking "why", it asks "*now what?*" The answer is *always* action — physical, psychological, or perspectival. The *Do Happy* framework will help you pull the arrow out by understanding where you want to go in the future, and taking actions towards it now, in the present moment. Once you pull out the arrow, you can throw it at a pinata of your choice. Let's get to work.

Part 1

The Theory

"Theory without practice is empty;
practice without theory is blind."
~ Immanuel Kant

This section explains what it means to *Do Happy* and emphasises the importance of feelings, thoughts, and actions. You will find that although each of these elements are important, they are not created equally. The opportunity to cultivate a delirious level of happiness exists in our ability to understand and leverage their differences. In particular, you will learn that the way forward is through the 3 P's of *action*: physical, psychological, and perspectival.

Chapter 1

What is Do Happy?

"Happiness depends upon ourselves."
~ Aristotle

How do you define happiness?

If you are like most, you will describe it as a *feeling*. Happiness is traditionally defined as a positive emotional state or *feeling* characterised by joy, contentment, life satisfaction, fulfilment, and peace.

Is it a nice definition? Yes.

Is it useful? No.

One of the biggest barriers to becoming happier lies in how we define it. Feelings are fleeting. They come and go. If you define happiness as a feeling, it also becomes fleeting. *This is unacceptable.*

Happiness is important and, if you're reading this book, you likely agree. I believe it is the *most* important thing, though I may be biased, considering I'm writing a book about it. If our happiness is so crucial, why leave it to chance?

What if instead of something that comes and goes, you are happy *all the time*? What would need to be true for this to be the case?

The Feel-Think-Do (FTD) model

To move towards answering this question, we need to understand the connection between what we FEEL, what we THINK, and what we DO. The Feel-Think-Do (FTD) model, fundamental to Cognitive Behavioural Therapy (CBT), explains this relationship (*See Fig 1*).

The model states:
1.   What we feel, affects what we think.
2.   What we feel, affects what we do.

Here's the cool bit:
3.   What we think, affects what we feel.
4.   What we think, affects what we do.

Here's the extra cool bit:
5.   What we do, affects what we feel.
6.   What we do, affects what we think.

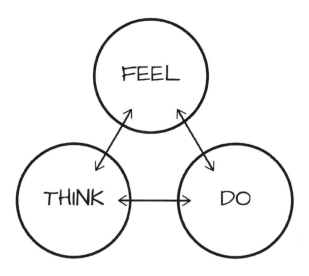

Figure 1 — CBT Model

What we FEEL, what we THINK, and what we DO are all linked and each of them affect each other.

When I see a patient or a client to discuss their mental health, which part of the model do you think they complain about? Almost always, it relates to an unpleasant *feeling*. They may be feeling stressed, anxious, worried, depressed, stuck, sad, overwhelmed, on edge, hopeless, or burnt out. Rarely do people make the connection between what they are feeling and their corresponding thoughts and actions.

As feelings, thoughts, and actions are all linked, it is valuable to cultivate awareness of this.

Feel = Depressed
Think = "This is never going to get better."
Do = Scroll on social media to escape the unpleasant emotions.

When someone is *feeling* depressed, they are likely *thinking* depression and *doing* depression as well.

Feel = Anxious
Think = "I am worried that I will embarrass myself."
Do = Avoid asking for a promotion.

When someone is *feeling* anxious, they are likely *thinking* anxiety and *doing* anxiety as well.

Feel = Happy
Think = "I am so grateful for my family and friends."
Do = Send a thank you note to a loved one.

When someone is *feeling* happy, they are likely *thinking* happy and *doing* happy as well.

What most people don't realise is that if they are *feeling* something, they are likely *thinking* and *doing* it too. The beautiful thing about the Feel-Think-Do model is that you can hack it. You can hack for happiness. In order to do this, we need to understand that although our feelings, thoughts, and actions are all linked, they are not created equally. The distinguishing factor? *Control.*

Can you control what you FEEL?

No. Tell a sad person to feel happy — what happens? If we could control our feelings, there wouldn't be a mental health epidemic. The model demonstrates that we can influence our feelings but we cannot control them.

Can you control what you THINK?

Yes and no. Thoughts can be unconscious or conscious. Our *unconscious thoughts*, the automatic and constant running commentary in our heads, *cannot be controlled*. If you try to control it, the less control you will have. It is like trying to hold a beach ball underwater. Eventually, you will lose your grip and the ball will come shooting to the surface. Our *conscious thoughts*, which are related to our ability to think with intention, *can be controlled*. For example, if I tell you to think of a fluorescent green elephant wearing high heels, can you? I bet you are picturing that glorious specimen right now! This is what I call *psychological action. Part 3* of this book will explore this further. There is also a deeper form of psychological action which I call *perspectival action,* which *Part 4* will cover.

Can you control what you DO?

Yes! Assuming physical capacity, if I tell you to stand on one leg and clap your hands, you can do it. This is what I call *physical action. Part 2* of this book will explore this further.

I mentioned earlier that when it pertains to one's mental health, most people complain about how they are *feeling*. If you can't control how you feel, why focus on it? It is like blaming yourself for the weather. Would you blame yourself if there was a storm outside? Of course not. It is completely outside of your control. You accept the weather as it is and dress appropriately. If it is a hot day, wear shorts and a singlet, and go to the beach. If it is raining, take an umbrella, wear a raincoat and drive safely because everyone becomes 79% worse on the road when it is wet.

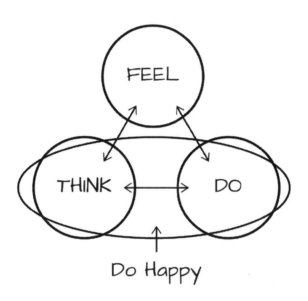

Figure 2 — Adapted CBT Model

As ridiculous as controlling the weather sounds, we try to do this all the time with our internal weather: our feelings. Instead, why not accept our feelings as they are and learn to "dress appropriately" by focusing on what you can control — physical, psychological, and perspectival action. Given that we cannot control how we feel, it becomes infinitely more powerful to focus on our *thinking* (psychological and perspectival action) and *doing* (physical action) (*See Fig 2*). Your feelings will take care of themselves. The difference between a happy person and an unhappy person is not just about how they are feeling. It has a lot more to do with what they are thinking and doing.

Happiness is a lot like spearfishing

Hatchet by Gary Paulsen recounts the survival journey of 13-year-old Brian who finds himself alone in the Canadian wilderness after surviving a plane crash while en route to visit his father. In order to survive, he learns how to spearfish. He fashions himself a spear, stands in the water and takes aim at the fish. Every time he thrusted his spear, he missed. Why?

Brian wasn't adjusting for the refraction of light. Once he adjusted for the light, he caught the fish. Happiness is a lot like spearfishing. We are often trying to "feel better". That is like aiming directly at the fish. We wonder why we so often "miss". Adjust for the light and instead aim at what you can control — *action* (physical, psychological and perspectival). In this subtle adjustment, you may "catch" what you have been looking for this whole time.

Happiness should be a constant. The way we make it a constant is by viewing happiness not as a feeling, but as a skill, a verb, an action and ultimately something that we *do*. Our ability to control what we do offers the biggest opportunity we have to transform our mental wellbeing. This is the fundamental premise of this book — shifting from trying to feel happy to doing happy.

Stop trying to feel happy, do happy instead.

Redefining happiness

Inevitably, when I encourage people to focus on their thoughts and actions, they misinterpret this to mean "ignore your feelings". That is *not* what I am saying. In the same way that you wouldn't ignore the weather outside (i.e. wearing shorts and a singlet in a storm), don't ignore the weather "inside" (i.e. trying to suppress unpleasant feelings like guilt or anger). As you will learn in the chapters to come, ignoring or suppressing your internal weather is a recipe for trouble. Regardless of the type of weather, outside or inside, all you can do is learn how to "dress appropriately" by focusing on what you can control.

Trying to ignore your feelings is a missed opportunity. Feelings are what allow us to have a full spectrum experience of life — the highs, the lows, and everything in between. Some feelings are pleasant — happiness, joy, pride, gratitude, contentment and peace. Some feelings are unpleasant — sadness, anger, depression, anxiety, worry and overwhelm. It is a normal part of life. It is a *beautiful* part of life.

We accept the weather as it is. We don't have a choice in the matter. Our feelings are similar. Whether you are feeling great or not, you can't control it. The *Do Happy* framework will help you learn how to "dress appropriately" for *any* type of weather you encounter, both externally and internally.

Russ Harris, in his book *The Happiness Trap*, describes happiness as a "rich, full and meaningful life". I would add a nuance:

Happiness =

The actions (physical, psychological and perspectival)
that contribute to a full, rich and meaningful life.

The actions that contribute to such a life are within our control. If we shift our definition of happiness to these actions and allow our feelings to naturally ebb and flow, then we move towards finding a way to be happy all the time.

Dr G's prescription

Cultivating a deep awareness of the connection *and* distinction between your feelings, thoughts and actions is a critical part of Doing Happy.

Turn to the corresponding page of your *Do Happy Workbook*, to complete the following exercise.

Pleasant feelings

1. Write down 3 pleasant feelings (e.g. happiness, joy, fulfillment, gratitude, compassion, excitement, peace, calm) that you have experienced recently in the FEEL column.

2. Write down the associated thoughts (all of them) in the THINK column.

3. Write down the associated actions (or inactions) in the DO column.

For example:

FEEL	THINK	DO
Happy	"I am really enjoying the time I spend with my family." "I am grateful that my parents put together such a feast." "I am so content with where I am in my life." "I am proud of how far I have come and I am excited by what the future holds."	I gave my child a hug and kiss. I am not using my phone. I was running around outside in nature with family and friends.

Unpleasant feelings

1. Write down 3 unpleasant feelings (e.g. anxiety, agitation, worry, depression, sadness, exhaustion, burnout) that you have experienced recently in the FEEL column.

2. Write down the associated thoughts (all of them) in the THINK column.

3. Write down the associated actions (or inactions) in the DO column.

For example:

FEEL	THINK	DO
Sad	"I can't believe that happened. How could they say something like that to me?" "Why does everything seem to go wrong for me?" "I feel worthless, like nothing I do matters." "I feel so alone, like no one really understands me."	Stay in my room. Social media binge.

You may have noticed that distinguishing between a feeling and a thought is harder than you expected. For example, sadness is a feeling but "I feel like everything is becoming too difficult" is a thought. Knowing the difference between a feeling and thought is crucial. We will cover this in more depth in the following section on *Speaking the Language*.

To make it easier for you, I have provided a list of feelings that you can choose from if you are struggling to put a name to your internal weather.

List of pleasant feelings

- Adventurous
- Awe
- Bliss
- Brave
- Caring
- Calm
- Capable
- Compassionate
- Confident
- Courageous
- Curious
- Delighted
- Daring
- Determined
- Ecstatic
- Eager
- Engaged
- Energised
- Enthusiastic
- Excited
- Empathetic
- Fulfilled
- Free
- Fortunate
- Fascinated
- Grateful
- Grounded
- Happy
- Hopeful
- Humbled
- Hopeful
- Inspired
- Invigorated
- Interested
- Intrigued
- Love
- Lively
- Lucky
- Moved
- Optimistic
- Patient
- Peaceful
- Playful
- Proud
- Passionate
- Radiant
- Refreshed
- Rejuvenated
- Renewed
- Satisfied
- Safe
- Serene
- Stimulated
- Strong
- Thankful
- Thrilled
- Touched
- Trusting
- Vibrant
- Vulnerable
- Warm
- Worthy

List of unpleasant feelings

- Afraid
- Aggravated
- Agitated
- Anxious
- Angry
- Anguish
- Annoyed
- Apprehensive
- Ashamed
- Bitter
- Bored
- Burnout
- Concerned
- Cranky
- Cynical
- Confused
- Depleted
- Despair
- Depressed
- Distant
- Disappointed
- Discouraged
- Dissatisfied
- Disturbed

- Edgy
- Empty
- Exhausted
- Frightened
- Frustrated
- Furious
- Gloomy
- Grumpy
- Grief
- Heartbroken
- Hesitant
- Hopeless
- Humiliated
- Impatient
- Indifferent
- Inhibited
- Incapable
- Insecure
- Irritated
- Isolated
- Lethargic
- Lonely
- Miserable
- Nervous

- Overwhelmed
- Panic
- Powerless
- Resistant
- Restless
- Sad
- Scared
- Self-conscious
- Shame
- Shocked
- Skeptical
- Sorrow
- Suspicious
- Teary
- Terrified
- Trapped
- Uneasy
- Unhappy
- Upset
- Useless
- Weak
- Weary
- Worn out
- Worried

Chapter 2

Speaking the Language

"Can I have some water?"
~ a thirsty Dr G in China

In 2013 my family went on a trip where almost no one spoke English. I vividly remember thinking I knew how to ask for water and confidently doing so, only to realise that I had the absolute wrong words. "Water? Bottle?" I asked desperately. I was met with sympathetic smiles. I had to become very good at charades.

When it comes to mental health, many of us struggle to speak the language. This can be an insidious barrier to our happiness because even though we may know the words, we often use them incorrectly. English vocabulary confuses the language of mental health. For example, we use the word "feel" interchangeably with things that are not feelings.

I feel sad. This expresses the feeling of sadness.

"I feel like you said that to hurt me." This is a thought, not a feeling.
"I feel hungry." This is physiology experience, not a feeling.

We have already explored the *Do Happy* model and its key components: feelings, thoughts and actions. It is essential to be able to understand the meaning of each component and to distinguish between them. This way, it won't feel like you are ordering water in a foreign country for the first time. Yes, that is not a feeling.

What is a feeling?

Finding a universally agreed upon definition of feelings was challenging — I consulted psychologists, reviewed journal articles, and searched extensively online, but couldn't find "the" answer.

What is a feeling?

I frequently ask this question when I am working one-on-one with someone or speaking to groups. Although the question is a simple one, the answers are often obscure. It is fascinating that despite often talking about our feelings, we can't reliably pin down what a feeling actually is.

To complicate matters further, what exactly is an *emotion*? Are they different to feelings? Some theories suggest that emotions are the physiological changes that occur in the body through the release of neurotransmitters and hormones by the brain, while feelings arise from the thoughts about those emotions. However, most people, including psychologists, use feelings and emotions interchangeably. I couldn't find any value in making the distinction between feelings and emotions, so I won't. If I use the word feeling or emotion, assume I am talking about the same thing.

Back to the question — *what is a feeling?* Here is how I define a feeling. My focus is not on what's right or wrong, but rather what's *useful*. Doing Happy requires that you can clearly distinguish between feelings, thoughts and actions and this definition helps you do that.

> *A feeling is a physical experience within the body that we label with our thoughts, depending on what is happening.*

Let's break this down.

A physical experience

Our feelings are always tied to physical experiences within the body. From the day we are conceived until the day that we die, our body is *constantly* undergoing physical changes. These bodily processes are governed by complex systems involving neurology (e.g. brain activity, neurotransmitters), endocrinology (e.g. hormones) and many other "ologies". The amazing thing is that through our five senses of sight, hearing, touch, taste, and smell, we can bring our awareness to some of these physical experiences.

These physical experiences, also called physiological experiences, include things like your heart rate (fast, slow, normal), breathing (rapid, shallow, deep), sweating, tingling, muscle tension, and pain. If you are sick, your physiology might become abnormal, such as experiencing shortness of breath during a chest infection. When you are not sick, it is useful to consider your physiology as a *neutral piece of data*. Rapid shallow breathing, for example, is just that — rapid shallow breathing. In the traditional sense, it is not yet what we would consider a feeling.

You may have noticed that the "Dr G's prescription" at the end of the previous chapter lists feelings as *pleasant or unpleasant*. When we consider the pleasantness of a feeling, it allows us to conceptualise our physical experiences as a neutral piece of data. It's either pleasant or unpleasant. That's not to say that it's good or bad, positive or negative. That is for the labelling and the context to decide.

Labelling with our thoughts

Our thoughts can be either conscious (i.e. intentional thinking) or unconscious (i.e. involuntary and automatic thinking). Once you bring awareness to your physical experience, you will notice that your thoughts almost automatically label that experience as a certain feeling. It is this labelling process that gives a name to what we call a feeling (see list of pleasant and unpleasant feelings in previous chapter). In *Part 3* of this book, you will learn how to utilise conscious thinking to transform how you are feeling.

For example, an increase in heart rate, sweaty hands and rapid shallow breathing may be labelled as anxiety or fear or excitement or any number of things.

How your mind labels the physical experience depends on...

What is happening

Depending on the context of what is happening, you will notice that what we traditionally consider a feeling will change.

For example, the physical experience may be an increased heart rate, rapid shallow breathing, dilated pupils and a tingling in the chest. In the context of waiting to speak on stage in front of 50 people, you may label this with your thoughts as fear. The same physical experience in a professional speaker about to spread a message close to their heart in front of 5000 people may label what they are feeling as excitement.

A racing heart and sweaty palms during a job interview might be labelled as anxiety. The same physical experience whilst reciting vows to your newly wedded wife might be labelled as love.

Someone with a clear mind and slow breathing during a meditation retreat may label their feelings as happiness and joy. The same physical experience in an elite athlete during competition could be labelled as flow.

In each of these examples, the same physical experience is labelled as different feelings depending on what is happening.

So what?

A feeling is a *physical experience* within the body that we *label with our thoughts*, depending on *what is happening*. Understanding the complexity of what comprises a feeling reinforces a key idea in this book, *you can't control your feelings*. You have very little control over your physical experience, your thoughts (the unconscious part), and what is happening.

While you can't control your feelings, deconstructing feelings into their three components: the physical experience, the labelling thoughts, and what is happening, allows you to separate yourself from your feelings. When you are able to observe something, you create a gap between "you" and what you are observing.

The ability to stand back and observe feelings for what they are provides a valuable insight: *you are not your feelings*. This is likely welcome news for people who believe otherwise. For example, just because you feel hopeless, it doesn't mean that you are hopeless. You are simply having a physical experience (e.g. persistent low energy), in the context of something that has happened (e.g. losing a loved one) and you are labelling it (e.g. as hopelessness).

The more we view feelings as a piece of data that we attach a label to, the more our relationship with those feelings will change. The concept of "positive" and "negative" feelings starts to dissolve. For example, feeling happy is not necessarily a positive experience and feeling sad is not necessarily a negative experience. It's just an experience.

If we are not our feelings, we can move away from defining true happiness as a feeling. In fact, in order to be happy and live a full, rich and meaningful life, you are guaranteed to encounter a *full range* of feelings — happiness, sadness and everything in between. That's normal, inevitable and I would add, *beautiful*. This sort of life, like a beautiful photo, is beautiful *because* of the contrast.

Dr G's prescription

Deconstructing feelings into its three components: the physical experience, the labelling thoughts, and what is happening, will allow you to observe feelings for what they are and separate yourself from them.

Turn to the corresponding page of your *Do Happy Workbook*, to complete the following exercise.

1. Write down three feelings. Ideally write them down as you are experiencing them. If you are having trouble putting a name to it, use the list of pleasant and unpleasant feelings in the previous chapter. *Note: What you are describing as a feeling has already been labelled with your thoughts, depending on what is happening.*

2. For each of these feelings, write down any physical sensations you are noticing (e.g. changes in your appetite, a fast or slow heart rate, rapid or slow breathing, pain, tension).

3. For each of these feelings, write down what was happening at
    the time (e.g. sitting in traffic, on a date, scrolling on your phone,
    receiving feedback from your boss).

Did you notice whether anything happened to your feelings as you
deconstructed them? Often, as you deconstruct a feeling, it forces
you to observe and separate yourself from them. You can see them for
what they are. This can often lead to a sense of peace and calm. We
will explore this phenomenon in future chapters. It's powerful and
fascinating stuff!

What is a thought?

Let's add another layer to our mental health vocabulary.

Thoughts are how we represent information in our minds.

Our ability to think is truly a miracle. The breadth of what we can think
about is even more astounding. Understanding our thoughts, how we
have them and in particular, distinguishing them from our feelings, will
help us *Do Happy* and take effective psychological action.

Figure 3 represents the full breadth of our ability to think — both in
content and *form*.

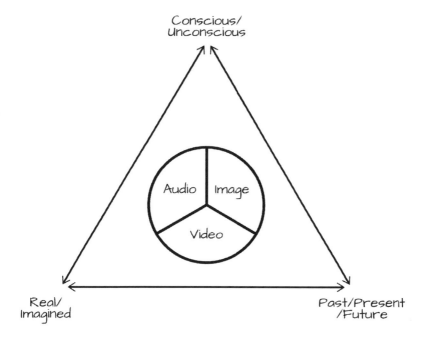

Figure 3

Content

The *content* of our thoughts is generated in three ways:

1. Conscious vs unconscious
2. Real vs imagined
3. Time: Past, present and future

Conscious thought is intentional and deliberate. Whether you are weighing up options to buy your first house, planning how you will propose to your partner or crafting a witty comment for a YouTube video, you are utilising conscious thought.

Unconscious thought is unintentional, automatic and spontaneous. It's the "little voice" that we all have in our heads. For many, this voice can be frustrating, constantly pointing out what's wrong with ourselves and the world around us. If you want to get to know the nature of your unconscious thoughts, find a quiet place, close your eyes and observe your mind wander like a child in a lolly store.

Real thoughts are based in objective facts and data. For example, thinking about Sri Lanka winning the cricket world cup in 1996 is a real thought because it actually happened.

Imagined thoughts are only limited by our imagination. Unfortunately, at the time of writing this, Sri Lanka winning another cricket world cup in the near future is only a figment of my imagination. Our ability to think about a pink dinosaur riding a skateboard is also an extreme example of what we can imagine between our ears.

Thinking can also vary depending on *time*. You can have thoughts about the *past*, the *present*, and the *future*.

Form

Our thoughts can also take 3 *forms*:
1. Audio
2. Image
3. Video

Audio represents the voice we hear in our head. However, the same thought can also appear as a picture or *image*. Similarly, this thought can take the form of *video*, much like a movie. For example, you may think, "I wish I was sipping on a dirty chai right now" (Audio). You could actually picture that beautiful beverage (Image). Perhaps you can see yourself drinking it (Video).

When you combine these variables relating to the *content* of our thoughts and the *form* which they take, you will realise that there is an *infinite* number of thoughts that our mind can create.

You can have *conscious/unconscious* thoughts, that are *real/imagined* about the *past, present or future*. Each of these thoughts can be in the form of *audio, images or video*.

In many ways, the world we live in is much smaller than the world between our ears. The type of world we create with our thoughts plays an immense role in living a happy life.

> *The world we live in is much smaller*
> *than the world between our ears.*

In the context of Doing Happy, we are most interested in our conscious thoughts because we can control them. This is where the opportunity for psychological action lies. *Part 3* of this book, *Intermediate Skills — Psychological Action*, explores this in detail.

Dr G's prescription

Understanding the nature of our thoughts and utilising our capacity to think is not only fascinating, it has the potential to transform every aspect of our lives.

Turn to the corresponding page of your *Do Happy Workbook*, to complete the following exercise.

Write down 5 thoughts you have in the next 10 minutes. Make a note of whether they are:

    a.   Conscious vs unconscious.

    b.   Real vs imagined.

    c.   Past, present or future.

    d.   Audio, image or video.

Thought	Conscious/ unconscious	Real/ imagined	Past/ Present/ Future	Image/ Audio/ Video
"I am going to be late for work."	Unconscious	Real	Present	Audio
Flashback of car accident.	Unconscious	Real	Past	Video
"I am such a failure."	Unconscious	Imagined (often perceived as real)	Present	Audio
Celebrating winning a premiership with your local sports team next weekend.	Conscious	Imagined	Future	Audio and video
Picturing your dream car.	Conscious	Imagined	Future	Image

I invite you to not overthink (pun intended) this exercise. The exercise is designed for you to get a grasp of the infinite diversity of our thoughts, not get the "right" answer. Have some fun with it.

What is an action?

It's time to add the final layer to our mental health vocabulary.

Actions refer to anything that we do,
or don't do, which we can control.

Doing happy incorporates the 3 P's of Action:

1. Physical
2. Psychological
3. Perspectival

Physical action is straightforward and refers to what we can do with our physical body. For example, slowing down our breath, cracking a joke like "9 out of 10 voices in my head tell me I'm crazy. The tenth is just humming", or belting out a full Taylor Swift concert in the car, represent physical actions. As long as our physical capacity allows, if we command our body to do something, it will comply. *Part 2* of this book, *Fundamental skills — Physical Action*, covers this in detail.

Psychological action, as discussed earlier, represents utilising *conscious thought*. Conscious thought is intentional and deliberate. Therefore, it is something that we can *do* and *control*. For example, choosing to see the positives in a difficult situation is a form of psychological action. *Part 3* of this book, *Intermediate Skills — Psychological Action*, covers this in detail.

Perspectival action is more abstract as it involves deeper thought patterns and core beliefs relating to how we perceive the world, ourselves and happiness. It is cultivated with conscious thought, reflection and contemplation and, eventually, it can become at least partly unconscious and automatic. For instance, the capacity to perceive beauty in extreme adversity, such as death, requires a fundamental shift in perspective. *Part 4* of this book, *Advanced Skills — Perspectival Action*, explores this in detail.

Doing Happy requires a *bias towards action*. Humans are wired to achieve results in their lives. There is only one thing that can directly influence the results in our life — *action*. Action, whether you do or don't do something, has consequences. Happiness, a life that is full, rich and meaningful is the ultimate result. You get there through the 3 P's of action.

Dr G's prescription

Doing Happy requires a bias towards action. Everything you will ever want in your life is on the other side of action — physical, psychological and perspectival.

Turn to the corresponding page of your *Do Happy Workbook*, to complete the following exercise.

1. Write down 3 examples of physical action that you have taken in the past 24 hours (e.g. sleep, exercise, take the train to work, study for exams).

2. Write down 3 examples of psychological action that you have taken in the past 24 hours (e.g. decide to order a wrap instead of a burger, plan in your head what you will wear to the party on Saturday night).

3. Write down 3 examples of perspectival action that you have taken in the past 24 hours. This would be an action that you have taken based on your core beliefs or deeply held perspectives. These actions may not seem obvious at first, but they stem from the values and principles you hold most dear. Look for situations where your actions were influenced by those beliefs, such as standing up for someone or something.

Now that you understand, and can distinguish between, three of the most important words relating to our mental health — feelings, thoughts, and actions — it's time to start Doing Happy.

Part 2

Fundamental Skills – Physical Action

*"Get the fundamentals down and the level
of everything you do will rise."*
~ Michael Jordan

If you want to dramatically and rapidly become happier, *physical* action is where you should start. These actions are referred to as the "fundamentals" because they are evidence based and apply to *everyone*. Happy people generally do the fundamentals well. If you are unhappy, it is highly likely that you are foregoing some, most or all of the fundamentals. These fundamental physical actions, if committed to on a regular basis, will solve most problems for most people. People are often looking for a fancy solution. It doesn't need to be fancy. If you are unhappy and you look at these fundamentals and realise that you are not doing most of them, this could be all you need. If you are already quite happy, you can use this section to better understand why things are going well for you and also look for areas of improvement.

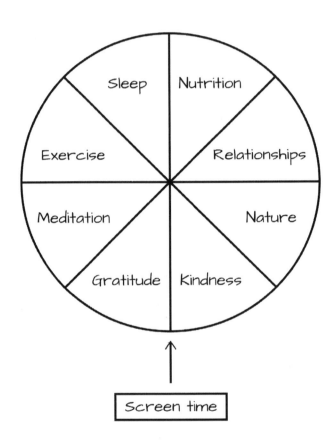

What are the fundamentals?

1. Exercise
2. Sleep
3. Nutrition

4. Relationships
5. Nature
6. Kindness
7. Gratitude
8. Meditation for focus
9. Replace screen time

We know that what we FEEL, what we THINK and what we DO are all linked. These nine fundamentals are the physical actions you can *do*, which you have direct control over, that will allow you to think and feel happier. It will also allow you to get some relatively quick yet significant wins.

The late Dr Stephen Covey once said, "common sense is not common practice." The fundamentals are simple. In practice, they are not easy. We all lead busy lives. It is easy to put things off. The fundamentals are usually first on the list.

» If work is demanding and stressful, you may sacrifice *sleep* by staying up late and waking up early.
» If you have kids, you may not make the time to *exercise*.
» If you are tired, you may eat high energy and low nutrition *foods* to get through the day.
» If you have tight deadlines, you may skip an important birthday and slowly sacrifice your *relationships*.

We all understand that these fundamentals are important. The problem is that they are *not urgent*. This means that they can wait, until they can't.

The non-urgent becomes urgent. As a doctor, I witness this first hand — a new diagnosis of type 2 diabetes, a heart attack, divorce, burnout or simply someone who is miserably unhappy. Doing Happy is about taking full ownership of your mental wellbeing. To do this, you need to find a way to make these life-changing fundamentals a part of your daily routine, ideally for the rest of your life.

Chapter 3
The Principles

"As to methods there may be a million and then some, but principles are few. The man who grasps principles can successfully select his own methods. The man who tries methods, ignoring principles, is sure to have trouble."
~ Harrington Emerson

There are three principles that can help you to implement the fundamentals into your daily routine:

1. Design for worst-case scenarios — Yes, MAM!
2. Consistency trumps intensity — The 3650 rule
3. Make it a big rock

Design for worst-case scenarios — Yes, MAM!

The single best time to implement the fundamentals of happiness is when everything is falling apart. If you design wellbeing routines that work on your worst day, it will work every day.

> *If you design wellbeing routines that work*
> *on your worst day, it will work every day.*

We often design wellbeing routines as if we were Goldilocks. Everything needs to be juuuuuuust right.

» *The weather needs to be good.* This eliminates more than half the year.
» *You are not too tired.* That window from when your coffee starts working to when it starts wearing off is a sacred one.
» *You have enough time.* A coaching client once told me, "I have been waiting 22 years for it to be the right time."

If we design wellbeing routines for near perfect conditions, we are doomed to fail. Design instead for worst-case scenarios.

Consider first aid. First aid is designed for when your heart stops beating. That is probably THE worst-case scenario.
Once you learn it, it's as simple as an acronym — DRSABCD.
Danger. Response. Send for help. Airway. Breathing. Circulation.

It works. First aid can be the difference between life and death.

First aid is not reliant on the weather, or whether you are tired or have time. It's a system that can be relied upon when everything is falling apart.

We need a similar system for our happiness. Do we have one? Yes, *MAM!* MAM stands for Minimum Absolute Must. MAMs form the foundation for each of our routines. A well-crafted MAM should seem frustratingly small and ridiculously easy to do.

For example,
Exercise: 1 push up.
Gratitude journaling: Write one thing that you are grateful for.
Meditation: 1 mindful breath.
Diet: 1 bite of a fruit.

A habit is something you do repeatedly and almost automatically with little conscious thought. The fundamentals need to become a habit. That's why having a MAM for each fundamental is crucial — it ensures that you can commit to these actions every single day, even on your "worst" day.

Having a MAM for each of your habits is a superpower for three reasons:
1. It's easy to do.
2. It's easy to do again and again.
3. It's easy to keep the habit alive on your "worst day".

It's easy to do

The hardest part of any routine is *starting*. A MAM helps to build consistency into the *start* of your habits. Think back to a time when you were tired and couldn't be bothered exercising but you did it anyway. Did you find that after you started, it was much easier to keep going? It is harder to get going than keep going. MAMs make it easier to start because they are designed to be frustratingly small and ridiculously easy to do.

It's easy to do again and again

This allows you to *build consistency into the start* of the habit. Having the discipline of MAMs keeps the habit alive and reinforces the mindset that you are someone who prioritises their happiness. Once the MAM is solidified, you can build intensity into your routines — meaning you can do more and do it for longer

It's easy to keep the habit alive on your "worst day"

Some days just suck. You get home and all you want to do is collapse onto the couch and wait for the day to be over. Don't accept defeat. Say Yes MAM! You can still do 1 push up (i.e. exercise related MAM) and then wait for the day to be over. If you can't consistently perform your MAM on your worst days, then your Minimum Absolute Must is probably not "minimum" enough. Make it even easier. Five minutes of meditation seems easy but many people find it hard to stick to, one mindful breath is a better MAM. Remember, a great MAM is frustratingly small.

Pro tip:
I strongly encourage you to design and experiment with MAMs for each of the fundamentals.

Consistency trumps intensity — The 3650 rule

When it comes to the fundamentals, I often see people prioritise intensity over consistency.

A classic example is exercise. You may know someone who wants to start exercising because they want to lose weight and feel better. In the midst of a wave of motivation, they book themselves into a 10-week boot camp. They go for 10 weeks, have some fun and risk injury. After that initial wave of motivation subsides, it's not uncommon for the exercise routines to disappear as well. The alternative is to make small daily commitments over the long term.

Happiness is a lifelong game. Therefore, the fundamental physical actions that contribute to your happiness need to be a lifelong commitment. I suggest aiming for *daily* and *forever*.

Do you see the value in doing something small, consistently?

The mathematics of small actions done consistently is too good to ignore. Introducing The 3650 rule.

The 3650 rule

Let's look at the difference a can of cola a day can make.

	1 can of cola a day	0 cans of cola a day
1 day	1	0
7 days	7	0
28 days (1 month)	28	0
365 days (1 year)	365	0
3650 days (10 years)	3650	0

A can of cola a day for 10 years is 3650 cans of cola. When you take into account that a can of cola typically has 10 teaspoons of sugar, that's 36,500 teaspoons of sugar after 10 years. Changing this one habit would result in two completely *different versions of the same person*: one who has consumed 36,500 teaspoons of sugar and the other, not. In the *Nutrition* chapter, you will discover how closely our food is linked to our mood.

Let's look at the difference a 10-minute run every day can make:

	10-minute run every day	0-minute run a day
1 day	10	0
7 days	70	0
28 days (1 month)	280	0
365 days (1 year)	3650	0
3650 days (10 years)	36500	0

A 10-minute run done every day amounts to 36,500 minutes of running after 10 years. That's 608.3 hours or 25.3 full days of running after 10 years. Compare this with zero. *Two completely different versions of the same person.* The only difference is a small daily action.

The only difference between a happy person and an unhappy person could be a handful of small, consistent daily actions.

Happiness comes down to mathematics.
The 3650 rule states that:

3650 X [Insert daily habit] =
The difference it will make in 10 years

3650 X 5 minutes of meditation every day = 18,250 minutes after 10 years. Ohmmmmm indeed.

3650 X 1 meaningful moment with a loved one *every day* = 3650 meaningful moments with loved ones after 10 years. The depth of the relationships you have with family and friends will sky rocket.

3650 X 1 wine bottle *every day* = 3650 bottles of wine. This would affect your mood and your liver.

3650 X writing down three things that you are grateful for *every day* = 10,950 things that you are grateful for. This would change the way you see the world.

> *"Most people overestimate what they can achieve in a year and underestimate what they can achieve in 10 years."*
> **~ Bill Gates**

When it comes to the fundamentals of happiness, consistency will always trump intensity.

Pro tip:

For each of the fundamentals, you can apply the 3650 rule to calculate the impact you can have with a small, consistent, and daily action over 10 years.

Make it a big rock

If you are a personal development geek like me, you will likely have heard this story.

A professor stood at the front of the class. He took out an empty jar and filled it with big rocks. He asked the class, "Is this jar full?" The class answered, "Yes." The professor then took a handful of pebbles and dropped them into the jar, shaking it gently so that the pebbles settled between the gaps made by the big rocks. He then asked, "Is the jar full now?" The class nodded with a smile, "Yes, *now* it is full." The professor then poured a cup of sand into the jar. The students watched as the sand filled around the rocks and the pebbles. The professor asked again, "Is it full now?" "Now it is definitely full," answered the students confidently yet hesitantly given they had already been wrong multiple times. The professor pulls out a jar of water. He pours the water into the jar until there is no remaining space left in the jar.

What was the professor trying to teach his students?

You can only put the big rocks in the jar if you put them first.

In the jar of life, the big rocks represent what's important to us. In order to live a ridiculously happy life, the fundamentals (e.g. exercise, nutrition, sleep, relationships, nature, kindness, gratitude, meditation and reducing screen time) need to be treated like big rocks that get put in your jar first. Whether it's checking our email, doom scrolling on our phone, binge watching our favourite streaming service or agreeing to meet with people we don't like, how often do we invest our limited time and energy on the pebbles, sand, and water of life at the expense of the big rocks?

If MAMs and the 3650 rule are about implementing the fundamentals, then the big rock analogy is about *making the fundamentals a priority*. Priority comes from the word prior, which means to come *before* something else. Don't take this in the literal sense. For example, trying to do all the fundamentals as soon as you wake up *before* everything else is usually not feasible. However, if I was to look at your calendar or observe your progress through the days, weeks, and months, would I be able to tell that the fundamentals are a priority for you?

Treat it like work

A practical way to understand this is to treat the big rocks, in this case the fundamentals, like work. Millions of people wake up every morning and go to work. You might wake up thinking "I'm too tired," "It's too cold," or "I can't be bothered today." Sound familiar? These are the same excuses people use to avoid sticking to their self-care commitments. Yet, somehow, most people still manage to go to work. Ever wonder why? Because work is *non-negotiable*. There are real consequences for skipping work. You can skip, but then you'll have to explain to your partner why you're using candles for light and why the family is having canned tuna again for the fifth night in a row.

Treat the big rocks like work.

My suggestion is to treat the big rocks in your life, in this case the fundamentals of happiness, like work. Once in a while you may "pull a sickie" but most days you will show up. If you have a job, you generally know when you start and finish. It is a part of your calendar. It is scheduled in. If someone asks you for something during these hours, you may respond with, "Sorry, I can't. I'm at work." This is the exact attitude and mindset I am advocating for with your big rocks. Make it a part of your calendar. Schedule it. I acknowledge that some things just don't make sense to schedule (e.g. random acts of kindness). That's okay. It's the principle that matters.

Make your fundamentals so important that if you are asked to shift your time and energy towards something else, you respond with "Sorry, I can't. I'm [insert fundamental here]." This will help you develop a very important skill, the ability to say "No." It's a beautiful word. In a world full of uncertainty, "No" is definitive. If you are like me and have an inclination to please people, saying "No" doesn't come naturally. With practice, it becomes easier. As soon as you say this magical word, you *immediately* free up time and energy that you can funnel into whatever you want, including the fundamentals. If you pass on something that would have taken two hours (e.g. a coffee with someone you don't like spending time with), you have two hours to invest in exercise, nature, quality relationships, meditation or any of the fundamentals. Treating your big rocks like work will make it a priority. This means that your happiness becomes a priority. If you are happier, you and everyone around you will benefit. Now let's get stuck into the Fundamentals of *Doing Happy*.

Chapter 4

Exercise

*"Only staying active will make you want
to live a hundred years."*

~ Japanese proverb

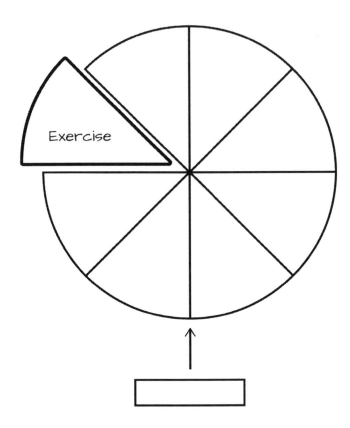

We want a magic bullet. We want a miracle cure to all of life's illnesses. We have something that comes close. It's called exercise.

I first met 23-year-old Henry with his concerned parents. Once social, happy and the "life of the party", Henry had lost his way over the past year. He was failing at university, isolating himself in his room and had become dependent on marijuana. His day mostly consisted of lying in his room, watching TV and smoking weed. It all came to a breaking point when a friend caught him stealing money. Henry was at rock bottom. The only reason he came out was to play soccer once a week for a local team.

When I met Henry and heard his story, we explored his fundamentals. *He wasn't doing any of them.* Here lay the biggest opportunity for Henry. Behaviour change is hard. It is infinitely harder when you are depressed. When things are tough, trying to change everything at once doesn't work. Henry decided that exercise would have the most impact. He loved soccer so we built his exercise routine around it. He started to see a rapid improvement in his mental wellbeing. Within four weeks, he was playing soccer twice a week and riding his bike every day. Henry was noticeably happier.

He didn't stop there. Exercise became a catalyst for positive change in all aspects of his life. He started to attend dinner at the dining table with his parents, he made an effort with his friends and started to have a regular sleep and wake time. Lastly, he threw out any marijuana he had left over along with his previously beloved bong. Within a few months, exercise became the first domino that set off a series of dominoes that gave him his life back. He still had his bad days, but overall he was back to being that social, happy person who was the life of the party.

Henry's transformation was not an accident. It was evidence based. Extensive research has undeniably confirmed the benefits of exercise on our mental health.

Key findings include:

- A systematic review by the University of South Australia, which assessed 1039 trials and 128,119 participants, found that: "physical activity is extremely beneficial to improve symptoms of depression, anxiety and distress".
- A study involving 15 European countries "found a positive association between physical activity and self-reported happiness".
- Research revealed "individuals who are physically active are happier. Further, individuals are happier in the moments when they are more physically active".
- Multiple studies have demonstrated that exercise, in some cases, is as effective as antidepressants and psychotherapy. There are numerous additional advantages for exercise over psychotherapy and medication, in terms of cost, side effects and physical health benefits.

Despite such strong evidence supporting the benefits of exercise for our mental health, Australians on average are not moving enough. As per the Australian Bureau of Statistics, in 2022, 94.4% of young people and nearly four in five (77.6%) of adults aged between 18-64 were not meeting the physical activity guidelines. For many people, exercise may be the single greatest lever they can pull to dramatically improve their mental and physical wellbeing. If you are unhappy, make exercise a *non-negotiable*. If you are happy, and if you haven't already done so, make exercise a non-negotiable. It doesn't matter who you are, the benefits are too good to ignore.

What to consider

When integrating exercise into your life, we need to consider the following:
1. Intensity
2. Frequency
3. Type and duration of exercise

Intensity

Light intensity: Requires minimal effort and does not significantly increase your heart rate or breathing rate. You can hold a normal conversation (e.g. household chores, gentle walk, gentle stretches, slow cycle).

Moderate intensity: Increases heart rate and breathing rate. You can just hold a conversation (e.g. a brisk walk, walking uphill, a light jog, cycling at a moderate pace, swimming at a moderate pace, dancing, and gardening — i.e digging and planting).

High or vigorous intensity: Increased heart rate associated with huffing and puffing. You can't hold a conversation (e.g. running, cycling at a fast pace, playing competitive sport).

Individual fitness levels affect how intense an activity feels. What might be low or moderate intensity for an elite athlete could be vigorous intensity for others.

Frequency

Being active is something that you need to do most days, preferably *daily*. In practice, *daily is easier*. Why? Because you won't succumb to decision fatigue. You only need to make the decision once. Once you decide, you don't have to negotiate with yourself on the days when you can't be bothered. It may not be feasible or possible to "properly" exercise every day. That's what our MAMs are for. If you can break a sweat and elevate your heart and breathing rate, it's a bonus. Make a commitment to move every day and try your best to keep it. It will change your life.

Type and duration

There are three main types of exercise.
1. Cardiovascular/aerobic exercise
2. Resistance exercise (i.e. strength training)
3. Flexibility

The following guidelines are suited to those aged 18-65.

Cardiovascular/aerobic exercise

The physical activity guidelines recommend that you aim for at least 150 minutes a week (2hrs 30 minutes) of moderate intensity activity or 75 minutes (1hr 15 minutes) of vigorous intensity activity a week.

Resistance exercise

Aim for at least two days a week per week on non-consecutive days to engage in muscle-strengthening activities (e.g. push-ups, pull-ups, squats, lunges, lifting weights). If you choose to do it daily, avoid working the same major muscle groups two days in a row.

Flexibility

Stretch (e.g. yoga) for 10 minutes 2-3 times a week. Doing it daily when your muscles are warm offers the greatest benefits.

> A few years ago, I was trying to run 5km in 20 minutes. My approach was to run as fast as I could every single time I ran. It was a simple strategy. It was also dumb. Once, I was on a jog and I ran past an elderly man. He was sitting on a park bench and smoking a cigarette. "All that exercise is going to kill ya," he called out. A few weeks later, I injured my calf. It took me months to rehabilitate. It didn't kill me but I learnt something very valuable: an injury can really

derail the momentum you build in an exercise habit. If you are new to exercise or planning to upgrade your 'routine, *get professional advice* (e.g. physiotherapist, exercise physiologist or personal trainer). Sometimes injuries are unavoidable, but investing time and energy into doing it safely is always worthwhile.

Specifics related to mental health

The following are specific evidence-based approaches that you can use to utilise movement to improve your mental health.

Consider what you need the most and choose exercises that align with those needs.
- All modes of physical activity, whether aerobic, resistance, mixed aerobic and resistance or yoga showed beneficial effects.
- Moderate to vigorous levels of activity (e.g. huffing, puffing, sweating) were better than low intensity (e.g. walking).
- Short to mid-duration bouts of exercise seem to be better than longer durations. All durations are effective though.
- Resistance exercise was better for depression.
- Yoga or a focus on mind-body exercises (e.g. walking) were more effective for anxiety.

You may have noticed that if you follow the physical activity guidelines, you will automatically touch on each of these.

Dr G's prescription

If there was a miracle cure for physical and mental illness, exercise would be a front runner. Aim to do it every day for the rest of your life.

Turn to the corresponding page of your *Do Happy Workbook*, to complete the following exercise.

1) Here is a summary of the physical activity guidelines that you can aim for.

- o *Cardiovascular/Aerobic exercise:* At least 150 minutes a week (2hrs 30 minutes) of moderate intensity activity or 75 minutes (1hr 15 minutes) of vigorous intensity activity a week.
- o *Resistance exercise:* At least 2 times per week engage in muscle strengthening activities.
- o *Flexibility:* Stretch (e.g. yoga) for at least 10 minutes 2-3 times a week.

2) Design a MAM for each. For example,

- o Jogging to the letterbox (Cardiovascular MAM)
- o 1 push up (Resistance MAM)
- o 1 downward dog pose (Flexibility MAM)

As you become comfortable with performing the MAM consistently on a daily basis, you can slowly do more. For example, after doing one push up every day for a week, two won't seem that hard. Whether you do 1 or 10, make sure you do at least one (i.e. the MAM) the next day.

3) Perform a 3650 forecast.

- o 3650 X 1 jog to the letterbox every day = 3650 small jogs after 10 years
- o 3650 X 1 push up = 3650 push-ups after 10 years
- o 3650 X 1 downward dog pose = 3650 downward dogs after 10 years

Chapter 5

Sleep

"Don't ask how people are doing, ask how they are sleeping. You'll learn a lot more."

~ Andrew Huberman

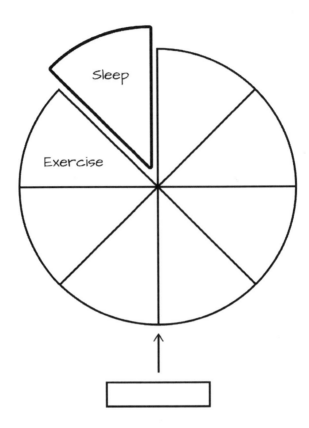

Sleep is a lot like playing guitar. If you haven't slept well, it can feel a lot like a tight guitar string. If you pluck a guitar string that has been stretched past its tensile strength, it will snap off the wood. When you don't prioritise sleep, you are like a tight guitar string. A "pluck" from someone or something is enough for you to snap. Prioritising sleep is like adding a little lax to the guitar string so that when life "plucks" you, you can maintain your peace and happiness. Here's what I know, if I have had a good night's sleep, everyone else becomes less annoying.

On a good night's sleep, everyone else becomes less annoying.

I have heard all the reasons why people don't prioritise their sleep:

» "I can sleep when I am dead."

» "Sleep is a waste of time."

» "There are more productive things to do than sleep."

» "I don't need much sleep."

» "I have too much to do so I just go to bed later or wake up earlier."

The same people who say these things are often stressed, exhausted and well, sleepy. How do I know? Because I am a recovering sleep-deprived person. After learning about and experiencing the benefits of sleep, I made it a *big rock*. I hope the same for you.

Sleep has been proven to improve physical, mental and emotional health. In a meta-analysis of 65 research trials consisting of over 8000 participants, it was found that "greater improvements in sleep quality [led] to greater improvements in mental health". The relationship between sleep and mental health was found to be dose responsive which means that for an improvement in sleep (i.e. the "dose" of sleep quality or quantity), there were improvements in the levels of depression, anxiety and stress.

Can you see why the fundamentals are so important? With these types of statistics, prioritising a good night's sleep may be all you need to *Do Happy*. Albert Einstein once called sleep an "absurdity" and predicted it would eventually be deemed useless and removed from our societal construct. However, mental health organization Beyond Blue reports that sleep-deprived individuals are "around 10 times more likely to experience depression." It seems Einstein didn't have this information. If you're still not convinced of sleep's importance, just ask a first-time parent.

In order to optimise your sleep, we need to focus on *quality* and *quantity*.

Quality of sleep

Improving your sleep quality can be achieved through better sleep hygiene. Sleep hygiene refers to the behaviours, routines and environmental factors that can be modified to ensure a better night's sleep. The following concepts and strategies will help you understand and improve your sleep hygiene, which will directly impact your day-to-day happiness.

Circadian rhythm

Our circadian rhythm, also known as our "body clock", dictates our cycle of sleeping and waking. There are two primary hormones that govern the circadian rhythm — cortisol and melatonin. In the morning, cortisol rises and melatonin is low or "suppressed". Over the day, as the body prepares itself for sleep, cortisol drops and melatonin rises (See Fig 4).

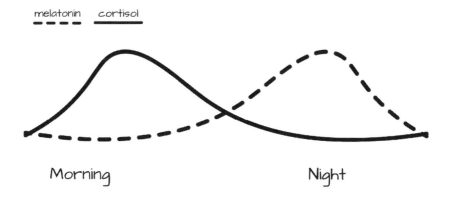

Figure 4

The following factors influence the circadian rhythm:
1. The intensity, spectrum and timing of light both natural (i.e. the sun) and artificial (i.e. screens, indoor lighting).
2. The regularity of sleep and wake times.
3. Caffeine intake.
4. Stress levels.
5. The intensity and timing of exercise.
6. Food intake, in particular carbohydrates, and its timing.
7. Fluid status and body temperature.

Each of the fundamentals mentioned in this book could be expanded into its own book. Instead of going into great detail on each of the points above, I am going to focus on the most common problems I see, which are usually related to *light, wake up times, caffeine and stress.* Of these factors, the number one factor is light. Light has more effect on your sleep than your high school crush had on your grades. Light intensity (i.e. lux), the light spectrum (i.e. wavelength) and the timing and duration of light all matter.

Light intensity and timing

Here is one of my favourite paradoxes:

Good sleep starts when you wake up.

We measure the brightness of light in *lux*. One lux is the amount of light emitted from a candle over a one metre radius.

All sources of light are not created equal:
- Bright sunlight at noon: 100,000 lux
- Cloudy day: 25,000 lux
- Overcast day: 2-10,000 lux
- Bright industrial lighting: 1-5,000 lux
- Offices and kitchens: 200-500 lux
- Household lighting: 50-200 lux
- Street lighting: 20 lux
- Full moon: 1 lux
- Computer screen: 0.5-37.8 lux
- Tablets: 0.7 to 5.9 lux
- TVs: 0.03 to 0.5 lux
- Smartphones: 0.6 to 2.1 lux

The brighter the light (i.e. more lux), the more likely it is to drive a cortisol spike and suppress melatonin. We want brighter light during the day, particularly in the morning, to spike our cortisol and suppress melatonin. This will increase alertness and decrease sleepiness during the day. We want dimmer light towards the end of the day to suppress cortisol and allow melatonin to rise. This will prepare the body for sleep.

Natural sunlight, even if it's overcast and cloudy, trumps any other form of artificial light. A cloudy day generates 25,000 lux whereas bright industrial lighting only generates up to 5,000 lux. It is hard to beat the sun in a brightness contest. Now, overlay this with the reality that we spend most of the day indoors. Again, good sleep starts in the morning with natural sunlight.

Light spectrum and timing

Looking at blue light from a screen is like starting a binge worthy Netflix special, it is risky to do it at night.

Light enters the eye through our pupils and strikes the inside surface of our eye known as the retina. The retina has light sensing cells called rods and cones. The rods detect light intensity (i.e. lux) and the cones detect the different wavelengths of light and, therefore, colour. Once the light hits the retina, it sends an electrical impulse to the brain. Blue light, once detected by the retina and then the brain, leads to the suppression of melatonin. Why does this matter? Because melatonin directly affects our circadian rhythm and therefore the quality of our sleep. Even at a low intensity for short durations, blue light suppresses melatonin and decreases sleepiness. Whilst this is acceptable during the day, it can significantly disrupt the quality of your sleep at night.

Before bed, less blue light means more good night.

So, what are the common sources of blue light? Conveniently, the sun is the biggest source of blue light. This further drives the case for morning sunlight exposure because you want to suppress melatonin in the morning. The main source of blue light in modern day society is of course digital screens such as smartphones, laptops, desktops, tablets and TVs. Screen time at night is a common culprit for poor sleep quality and quantity.

Dr G's prescription

Light, in particular sunlight, is the primary driver of our circadian rhythm. Improve your relationship with light by maximising sunlight exposure in the morning and minimising blue light exposure at night.

1. **Get 15 minutes of direct morning sunlight exposure.**

It doesn't matter if it is cold or cloudy as the brightness of the light, which is what spikes cortisol and suppresses melatonin, is still better than indoor lighting.

Pro tip:

Eat breakfast outside, go for a morning walk or read a book outside in the morning to stack another useful habit onto your morning sunlight exposure.

2.   **Turn off screens 90 minutes before sleep.**

This means everything — smartphones, laptops, desktops, tablets and TVs. Fill these 90 minutes with something that helps you wind down (e.g. a bath, play an instrument, read a book, talk to your partner).

Pro tip:

Get an old school analogue clock so you don't have to set an alarm on your phone before sleep.

Wake up time

Our body clock is guided more by our wake-up time than our bedtime. Our wake-up time puts the rhythm in circadian rhythm. Many of us sleep late and wake up early during the weekdays and sleep in on the weekend. Naturally, this makes Monday a painful experience. Dr Jason C. Ong, sleep scientist and author of *Mindfulness-based therapy for insomnia*, advocates for a *consistent wake up time*. This means that if you wake up at 6am during the week, doing the same on the weekend will regulate your body clock and enhance your sleep quality. The most common problem with keeping the same wake-up time is the accumulation of sleep dept during the week. By the weekend, people need a rest. Try to keep a consistent wake up time but go to bed earlier. This will allow for both sleep quality *and* quantity.

Dr G's prescription

Pick a suitable wake up time and try to consistently get out of bed within the same 15-minute window. If you are tempted to sleep in, keep the same wake up time and go to bed earlier.

Caffeine

There are two types of people: people who drink coffee and people who are grumpy because they haven't had their coffee. Coffee, and other caffeine containing products such as tea and energy drinks, are ingrained in our culture. For many, although it is performance enhancing and increases alertness, it can lead to poor quality sleep. In a systematic review that examined the effect of caffeine on sleep, caffeine consumption was shown to "reduce total sleep time by 45 minutes and sleep efficiency by 7%". Caffeine can create a vicious cycle. Caffeine affects our sleep quality and quantity. We are subsequently tired during the day and therefore consume caffeine which once again, compromises sleep.

We can still enjoy caffeine as long as we understand and respect how long its effects last. Individual sensitivity to caffeine varies from person to person. You probably know someone who can't even have a sip of coffee as they will be left wide-eyed at night and on the other extreme, the person that can drink a coffee just before sleep with no issues. In general, caffeine's effects can last between 2 to 12 hours. If you struggle with your sleep and you consume caffeine, cutting it out or enforcing a curfew may significantly improve your sleep quality.

Dr G's prescription

To improve sleep quality, less caffeine and having it earlier is better. Have your caffeine intake a *minimum* of 8 hours before bed time. For example, a 10pm bedtime means no caffeine after 2pm. If you think that you are hypersensitive to caffeine, avoid it altogether or have it as early in the day as possible.

Stress

Stress can induce a fight-or-flight response which releases cortisol and adrenaline into your bloodstream. This can disrupt your circadian rhythm. Alongside this physiological response, stress is also associated with a "racing mind" which most of us have all experienced at some point in our lives at three in the morning. According to an American Psychological Association survey, people who had lower stress levels slept an average of 7.1 hours compared to 6.2. Who wouldn't want an extra hour of sleep?

Dr G's prescription

It is difficult to recommend a specific strategy to reduce stress levels at night as there are so many. In fact, *all* the strategies in this book can help to lower stress levels. If high stress and poor sleep are issues for you, all I can say is to make alleviating stress a priority. If in doubt, exercise (ideally outside and in the morning) and meditation (before sleep) are great places to start. Alternatively, given sleep deprivation itself is a common source of stress, going to bed earlier may be the solution.

Quantity of sleep

According to the Australian Institute of Health and Welfare, "in 2018, one quarter of 12-13 year olds (27%) and half of 16-17 year olds (52%) were not meeting sleep guidelines on school nights." On average, Australian adults aged between 18 and 65 were sleeping approximately 7 hours.

How much is enough?

General sleep requirements for adults typically range between 7 to 9 hours per day. However, this can vary significantly from person to person based on individual needs and age. See the table below.

SLEEP DURATION RECOMMENDATIONS		
Age Group	**Age Range**	**Recommended Amount of Sleep Per Day**
Newborn	0-3 months	14-17 hours
Infant	4-11 months	12-15 hours
Toddler	1-2 years	11-14 hours
Preschool	3-5 years	10-13 hours
School-age	6-13 years	9-11 hours
Teen	14-17 years	8-10 hours
Young Adult	18-25 years	7-9 hours
Adult	26-64 years	7-9 hours
Older Adult	65 years or older	7-8 hours

Source: www.sleepfoundation.org

Dr. Matthew Walker, founder and director of the Center for Human Sleep Science, offers an intriguing perspective on the timeless question of optimal sleep duration. He suggests that adults should have "about 90 minutes more than they are already getting," which corresponds to approximately one complete sleep cycle. This is an insightful and practical answer because the reality is that most of us are walking around sleep deprived.

In order to understand why an additional sleep cycle is beneficial, we need to understand the four stages of sleep and in particular, Non-REM vs REM sleep.

Non-REM vs REM sleep

A· sleep cycle consists of four sleep stages which each last about 90 minutes. This is non-REM (rapid eye movement) sleep.

Stage 1: The shallowest stage of sleep where you still have drifting thoughts and can be easily woken up.

Stage 2: This is a moderate stage of sleep characterised by unique brain activity and being slightly harder to be woken up.

Stage 3 and 4: These are the deepest stages of non-REM sleep, characterized by unique brain activity and the greatest difficulty waking up from.

REM sleep: This stage begins approximately 90 minutes after falling asleep. It is characterised by rapid eye movements (REM) and increased brain activity. Dreaming primarily occurs during this stage, and there is concurrent paralysis of major voluntary muscle groups to prevent acting out dreams.

See Figure 6 to see the sleep cycles in a healthy younger person:

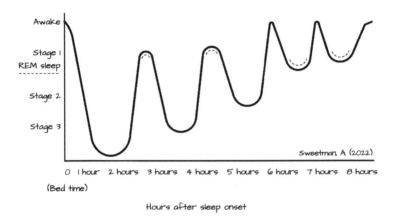

Figure 6: Healthy younger person's normal sleep

See Figure 7, to see the sleep cycles in a healthy older person:

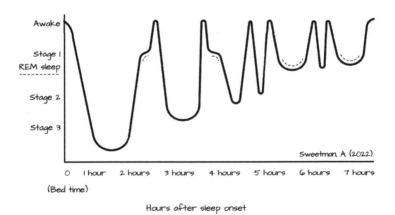

Figure 7: Healthy older person's normal sleep

It is important to understand the benefits of Non-REM and REM sleep. It is a complex topic that I have attempted to simplify.

Non-REM sleep aids physical recovery and memory.
REM sleep aids with emotional balance, memory, and cognition.

In a book about happiness, the implications of REM sleep on emotional balance offer an exciting opportunity. This is where the importance of sleep quantity comes into play. Look closely at Figure 6 and Figure 7, what do you notice about the duration of the REM sleep as you progress through the night?

REM sleep is proportionately greater in the later stages of sleep. Conversely, non-REM sleep is greater in the earlier stages of sleep. Why does this matter? Let's say you normally sleep for 8 hours. However, one night you sleep for only 6 hours. How much sleep did you lose? In absolute terms, you slept 2 hours less. However, you may have lost approximately 50% of your REM sleep as sleep cycles are not created equally. The benefits of sleep at the beginning of the night are very different from those you experience toward the end.

Most of the REM sleep occurs in the later stages of sleep.

Considering the alarming mental health statistics, the prevalence of sleep deprivation, and the role REM sleep plays in emotional regulation, the conclusion is clear: *sleep for an additional 90 minutes.*

Dr G's prescription

If you are not getting enough sleep, aim to go to bed earlier. If you manage to get to bed 90 minutes earlier every night, that's an extra 10.5 hours of sleep a week! If you are sleep deprived, every extra hour of sleep will significantly boost your wellbeing and productivity.

Turn to the corresponding page of your *Do Happy Workbook*, to complete the following exercise.

There are many ways to improve your sleep and I have given you multiple "prescriptions" in this chapter.

1. **Choose *one thing* that you think will have the most impact.**
   o It may be getting morning sunlight, reducing screen time at night, cutting out coffee or going to bed earlier.

2. **Design a MAM for each. For example,**
   o Instead of 15 minutes of morning sunlight, you could start with 30 seconds.
   o Instead of 90 minutes of no screen time before bed, start with 2 minutes.

3. **Perform a 3650 forecast.**
   o Consistent small changes make a big difference over time. Your consistency will allow you to naturally scale up these routines.
   o 3650 X 30 seconds of morning sunlight every day = 109,500 seconds (1825 minutes or 30.4 hours) of morning sunlight after 10 years.

o 3650 X 2 minutes less screen time every night = 7300 minutes (121.7 hours) less screen time at night after 10 years.

Chapter 6

Nutrition

"Let food be your medicine and medicine be your food."
~ Hippocrates

Alternatively, "Poo-poo is a sometimes food."
~ Kin (6-year-old boy)

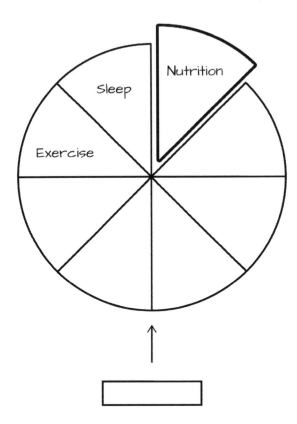

How many brains do we have? What if the answer is *two*?

The first brain is *the* brain. It is the one that sits between our ears. The engine that drives everything. It keeps us alive and is like the puppeteer behind everything that we feel, think and do. It's responsible for curly fries, self-driving cars, artificial intelligence and mean YouTube comments. This is our *central nervous system*.

The second brain is not as well known. It is *the gut*. The long and windy journey from our mouths, where food goes in, to our rectum, where poo comes out, is lined with millions of nerve cells. This is our *enteric nervous system*. Colloquially, at least at an intuitive level, we seem to accept the gut as our second brain. For example, when making a big decision, do you listen to your brain or "go with your gut?" When you are nervous, you may have a racing mind but you may also get "butterflies in your stomach".

The gut-brain axis

The enteric nervous system and the central nervous system form the *gut-brain axis*. It is like having numerous interconnected highways between two capital cities, the brain and the gut, which allows you to send messages back and forth. The gut and the brain are constantly communicating with each other. The belief that the brain solely controls the body and the gut is only responsible for digestion is now outdated.

The Food and Mood centre at Deakin University is a world-leading research centre in Australia that aims to understand the way in which what we eat influences our brain, mood and mental health. Their research, along with findings from different parts of the world, is adding to a growing body of evidence that *the brain influences activities in the gut and the gut influences activities in the brain* (See Figure 8). For example, mood disorders such as anxiety and depression have been linked to disruptions in gut function that may present as reflux, nausea, abdominal bloating, excessive gas, constipation or diarrhoea. Similarly, diseases of the gut, such as irritable bowel syndrome, are linked with psychological distress and an alteration of the gut microbiome.

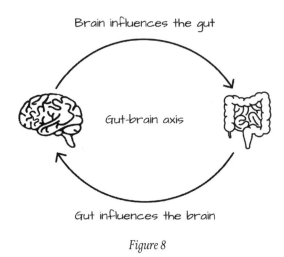

Figure 8

The gut microbiome

Trillions of microorganisms, also known as "bugs", live in your gut. They are mostly bacteria, but there are also viruses, yeast, fungi and parasites. These microorganisms form your *gut microbiome*. There are at least as many bugs in our gut as there are human cells in your body. We are more bug than human. If you are a germaphobe, my apologies.

We are more bug than human.

The composition of our gut microbiome, which refers to the types and number of bugs living in our gut, appears to profoundly influence not only gut health, but also brain health, cognition and mood. There is evidence to suggest that when our gut microbiome is unhappy, it can affect our mood and can even be linked to anxiety and depression., Numerous studies have also shown that changes in the gut microbiome affect how various neurotransmitters are made. One such neurotransmitter is serotonin. Most antidepressants work by boosting the levels of serotonin in the brain. What's fascinating is that approximately 90% of serotonin is actually made in the gut. Although a finding like this is compelling, it is worth noting that the serotonin made in the gut doesn't seem to be able to enter the brain. Nevertheless, the research in this field is growing and it is very promising. I am not a betting man but I would bet the house that the *trillions* of bugs that live in our gut do a lot more than watch food pass by.

So how do we improve our gut microbiome? By paying attention to what we eat and drink.

What we consume directly impacts the gut microbiome. Since our gut is linked to our mental health, what we eat and drink also affects our mental well-being.

How often do we point to our diet when we are
struggling with our mental health?

In a world where many people struggle with their mental health and also have poor diets that are high in energy and low in nutrients (e.g. ultra-processed foods like sugary drinks), the potential for better nutrition to improve mental health is exciting.

What should we consume

> Once a friend called me in distress.
> "I stuffed up."
> "What's up?"
> "I put the wrong petrol in my car."
> "Just drive it and see what happens." (This is why I look after people and not cars)
> "Well, it can damage the engine."
> "What are you going to do?"
> "I'm waiting for this guy to come and pump the petrol out of the car"
> "There's a guy for that?!?!"

Our bodies are a lot like cars. We need to put in the right fuel. Thankfully there's a "guy". Let that guy be Michael Pollan. In his book, *Food Rules: An Eater's Manual*, he informs us in 7 words how to eat healthy.

"Eat food. Not too much. Mostly plants."

I would add 3 more words:

Eat food. Not too much. Mostly plants. Hydrate. Avoid drugs.

Follow the principles behind these 10 words *most of the time for the rest of your life*, and you will certainly have a healthy diet. Nutrition is one of the most contentious topics in the health industry. Whether it's fasting, a ketogenic diet, a Mediterranean diet, a plant-based or vegan diet, a gluten-free or dairy-free diet, a low-FODMAP diet, an anti-inflammatory diet, or any of the numerous others, it can be complex and overwhelming to navigate. In times of complexity, I value simplicity. These 10 words are evidence-based and common sense, though they are far from common practice.

Eat food

Pollan advocates for eating "real" food, which is the kind of food that our great grandparents would recognise. The closer the food is to its natural state, such as being plucked from a tree, pulled from the earth or found roaming in nature, the better it is for your mental and physical wellbeing. Research shows that a nutrient dense diet, rich in real foods, can reduce the risk of a major depressive disorder. Unsurprisingly, diets that are high in ultra-processed foods are associated with an increased risk of depressive symptoms.

Spotting processed foods

Processed food refers to any food or drink that has been *changed* in some way before it reaches the consumer. Anything in a box, a bag or a container is processed. Not all processing is bad; some foods need it for safe consumption. For example, raw cow's milk contains harmful bacteria, so it's pasteurised and bottled to make it safe. Milk is *minimally processed* as it remains close to its original form. We need to be mindful of foods and drinks that are *heavily or ultra-processed*. These products, often made in factories, are processed to enhance taste, shelf life and ultimately, profitability. They rarely offer any health benefits.

The following 3 questions will help you determine whether a food is processed, and, if so, whether it is minimally or heavily/ultra-processed.

1. **Does it come in a box, bag or container?**
   If the answer is yes, it is processed.

2. **Does it look "real"?**
   If your great grandparent would recognise it as "real" and appearing like its original form (e.g. milk), then it will be minimally processed. A bag of snakes (a type of lolly) doesn't look anything like a real snake and is therefore heavily/ultra-processed. Even if you turn your head a bit and squint, you won't be able to find a whole food that looks even remotely like it.

3. **How many ingredients does it have?**
   The more ingredients it has and, in particular, the more ingredients you don't recognise or wouldn't stock in your pantry, the more processed it is. For example, if you see emulsifier 222 and preservative 125 on the list, you are in trouble.

   What happened to the first 221 emulsifiers anyway?

Pro tip:

If it is heavily or ultra-processed (e.g. sugary drinks, most breakfast cereals, snack foods, processed meats), minimise its consumption. Unfortunately, they are everywhere so it is easier said than done.

The specifics

Here are specific recommendations by the Food and Mood centre at Deakin University that will help you to "Eat Food":

· Limit ultra-processed foods and replace them with minimally processed foods.

· Aim for a high consumption of foods rich in omega-3 polyunsaturated fatty acids, such as certain fish and seafood (e.g. salmon, sardines, herring, mackerel, anchovies, tuna), nuts (particularly walnuts), seeds (e.g. chia seeds, flax seeds) and green leafy vegetables.

· Consume red meat (e.g. beef, pork, lamb) in moderation. Opt for lean sources rather than fatty/processed cuts.

Pro tip:

Often, we don't want to "deprive" ourselves. Instead of focusing on reducing processed foods, focus on increasing real foods.

Not too much

You enter your favourite restaurant and order a mouth-watering steak, crunchy chips, and salad. The meal looks enormous as the waiter brings it out. You lunge in for your first bite. Your taste buds have never experienced this much euphoria. Halfway through, you start feeling full but push on, thinking, "What about the starving kids? Do it for them." By this stage, it is difficult to appreciate the taste. It is all about the starving kids at this point. You succeed. The plate is empty. Bloating and regret become your reality for the next few hours.

Hara hachi bu is a Japanese saying that instructs us to stop eating when we are 80% full. Traditional Chinese medicine has a similar saying, "Only eat 70 percent full, and wear 30 percent less." According to the Australian Bureau of Statistics, as of 2022, almost two thirds (65.8%) of adults are overweight or obese. On average, we eat too much and too often. Research suggests a two-way relationship between excessive weight and mental health issues, with depression increasing the risk of obesity and vice versa.

Pro tip:

Eat slowly. Food is awesome so why rush it? When you are 80% full, it's OK to stop. Save it for later or put it in the rubbish bin, otherwise you become the bin.

Mostly plants

The World Health Organisation (WHO) suggests that low fruit and vegetable intake is the 12th leading risk factor for dying. Consuming stuff that is grown from the earth, a more plant-based diet, has been shown to improve the quality of our gut microbiome and therefore, our mental wellbeing and happiness.

The specifics

Specific recommendations by the Food and Mood Centre at Deakin University that will help you eat "Mostly plants":

- Increase the consumption of fruits, vegetables, legumes (e.g. peas, beans and lentils), wholegrains (e.g. brown rice, wholegrain bread, oats), nuts, seeds, herbs and spices.
- High consumption of fibre which is the indigestible part of plants (e.g. fruits, vegetables, wholegrain foods).
- Use extra virgin olive oil as the main source of cooking oil. This is the "highest grade" form of olive oil.

Pro tip:
The Australian Dietary Guidelines recommend five servings of vegetables a day. To make it more practical, aim for five handfuls of vegetables daily.

Hydrate

We are 60-80% water, yet we often neglect it as a crucial nutrient. Many of us walk around dehydrated which affects both physical and mental wellbeing. When I don't have enough water, the "G" in Dr G stands for *grumpy*.

The specifics

Specific recommendations by the Food and Mood Centre at Deakin University that will help you "Hydrate":

- Men need approximately 2.5L (10 cups) a day
- Women need approximately 2L (8 cups) a day.

Pro tip:

Get a large 2-3L bottle and fill it up at the start of the day. Finish it by the end of the day. Alternatively, keep drinking until your urine looks like water.

Avoid drugs

People with mental health conditions or high levels of psychological stress are more likely to engage in risky behaviours, including drinking alcohol excessively, smoking (twice as likely), and using illegal drugs (1.7 times more likely). Alcohol in particular, despite being considered a drug, is an ingrained aspect of society and culture. Alcohol works as a "depressant", and slows down communication between your brain and body, affecting how you feel, think and act.

The specifics

Specific recommendations by the Food and Mood Centre at Deakin University that will help you "Avoid drugs" are self-explanatory:

- Avoid excess alcohol consumption.
- Avoid smoking and illegal drugs.

Pro tip:

This is a contentious topic. If you are struggling with your mental health and you consume alcohol, smoke or take illegal drugs, consider stopping for one month to see if it helps. If you can't stop for a month, then you may have a different problem.

Dr G's prescription

A healthy gut microbiome is associated with improved mental wellbeing. What we eat and drink directly impacts our gut.

Turn to the corresponding page of your *Do Happy Workbook*, to complete the following exercise.

1. **The following 10 words will help you immediately improve the quality of your nutrition:**
   - Eat food. Mostly plants. Not too much. Hydrate. Avoid drugs.
   - Pick *one* of the concepts to focus on.

2. **Design a MAM. For example,**
   - Before you buy a food/drink, ask "Does it come in a box, bag or container?" (Eat real food MAM).

o Eat one bite of a fruit every day (Eat real food/Mainly plants MAM).

o If you feel full, ask "Am I 80% full?" (Not too much MAM).

o Drink one cup of water as soon as you wake up (Hydrate MAM).

o If you are stressed, and are about to pour yourself some wine, go outside and take three deep breaths (Avoid alcohol/drugs MAM).

As the MAM becomes consistent on a daily basis, you can slowly do more. For example, one bite of a fruit can become the whole fruit.

3. **Perform a 3650 forecast:**

o 3650 X 1 bite of a fruit every day = 3650 bites after 10 years.

o 3650 X 3 deep breaths (instead of a glass of wine) = 10,950 deep breaths and potentially 3650 less glasses of wine after 10 years.

Chapter 7

Relationships

"The people who were happiest, who stayed healthiest as they grew old, and who lived the longest were the people who had the warmest connections with other people"
~ Robert Waldinger

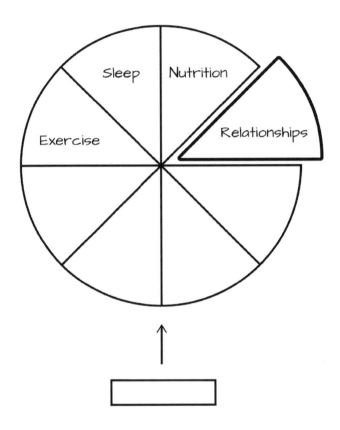

The Harvard Study of Adult Development is the longest study on happiness. It has studied what makes people live long and happy lives for over 80 years. The study started in 1938 during the Great Depression when 268 Harvard sophomores, all men, had their health tracked to determine what leads to a healthy and happy life. Over the decades, the research has expanded to include children and women.

The research revealed every aspect of the human condition. Some participants became doctors, lawyers or successful businessmen.

One participant, John F. Kennedy, was a bit of an overachiever, he became the president of the United States of America. Conversely, some developed schizophrenia or developed alcohol addictions. Given the study has been going for over 80 years, many of the participants and the original researchers have died.

So, what's the verdict?

Quality relationships matter.

It turns out that close relationships, more than money or fame, keep people happy throughout their lives. The perceived satisfaction of the relationships that people have with their family, friends and community is paramount. A happy life is built with good relationships. Lead researcher of the study Robert Waldinger has found that "it's not just the number of friends you have, and it's not whether or not you're in a committed relationship, but it's the quality of your close relationships that matters." Conversely, the findings of the study suggest that "loneliness kills... it's as powerful as smoking or alcoholism."

If you want to observe the impact that loneliness can have on someone's happiness, visit a nursing home.

> I used to look after a nursing home resident who was grumpy, miserable and rude. That's not what upset me. What upset me was that no one ever visited him. No family. No friends. When he died, his son

visited the nursing home out of the blue. He wasn't grieving. He came to ask me whether his Dad had any hereditary medical problems he should be worried about. I don't know if loneliness killed his Dad, but it definitely made him very unhappy.

The challenge we face is that we live in a fast-paced world that glorifies productivity and high output. Society rewards high performance. We get a pat on the back when we make more money, finish a challenging work project or move into a beautiful house. Society doesn't care if you had a nice dinner with your best mate, surprised your wife with an axe throwing experience (true story), or went on a walk with your Mum. I want you to hear this loud and clear: research, common sense, and experience all agree — *it is never a waste to invest time, energy, and money into cultivating deep and meaningful relationships with others.*

I recently spent some quality time with some quality people: my wife, sister-in-law, and mother-in-law. We watched a Hindi movie called Dhak Dhak which was about a group of women who set out on an adventure of self-discovery. It had an interesting take on the age-old conversation of whether it is the journey or the destination that matters. I have always been a "journey" guy. In the movie, they commented that it is neither the destination or the journey, but rather the company you keep on your journey. My wife and I instinctively looked at each other and exclaimed, "I love that!"

The two multipliers

Cultivating quality relationships is a "big rock". For some people it comes naturally, for others, like any skill, it can be learnt. I have found the following two multipliers have helped me to create depth in my relationships with family, friends, and the wider community:

1.   Quality conversations are a multiplier.
2.   Quality time is a multiplier.

Quality conversations are a multiplier

Quality conversations require you to be interesting. As Dale Carnegie said, "To be interesting, be interested." To be interested, ask questions and listen. I love well-crafted questions because they often lead to deep and meaningful conversations.

Good questions give good answers.
Great questions can change your life.

Here are five principles to consider when asking questions and listening. They will help you to cultivate quality conversations and thus, quality relationships.

1. Avoid close-ended questions

Close-ended questions encourage one-word answers like "yes", "no", "good" or "bad". For example, "Did you have a good day?" "Yes." These types of questions are like a stop sign on the road to quality conversations.

2. Ask open ended questions

Open-ended questions encourage interesting answers. Try it out by starting the question with the following words: why, how, what, describe or tell me about.

As I speak regularly on the topic of happiness, I was asked to facilitate open dialogue between two groups of people — parents and children. Through the power of open-ended questions, more than 100 people joined in and co-created a moving and memorable experience. Parents spoke about how they have cheated on tests, met the love of their life in high school and even did a "runner" after having a meal at a restaurant. Their children shared stories about changing their report card to fool their parents and how they took their first sip of alcohol. A few detailed very difficult periods in their life that even their loved ones didn't know about. These were truly *quality conversations*. Within a few hours, these conversations strengthened relationships and forged new ones. It all started with open-ended questions.

If you are new to open-ended questions, do some research online to see what questions you can add to your arsenal. Here are some open-ended questions that I have found to be useful in igniting incredible conversations:

- What is occupying your mind these days?
- What is the best thing that has happened to you in the last week?
- Why did you [insert decision/behaviour that intrigued you]?
- What are you working towards?
- Is there anything that is bothering you? Tell me about it.
- I noticed that you went through a really difficult period. How did you get through it?
- What's the biggest challenge in your life at the moment?

3. After you ask the question, shut up

After you ask the question, *shut up*. Let the silence do the heavy lifting. Humans are wired to fill the silence. If you don't fill it, the person you are talking to will. Listen carefully to what the person is saying. Try to understand their world. In that moment, make them the most important person in your world.

4. Listen actively

Active listening requires that you ask follow up questions that are *relevant* to what is being talked about. Be curious. Don't just wait for them to stop so you can say what you want to say. That's not listening. As Dale Carnegie said, "first seek to understand, then to be understood".

5. Withhold judgement, unless it is asked for

This may be the hardest part. Quality conversations require vulnerability. Vulnerability means *opening yourself to judgement*. For this to occur, the person needs to feel psychologically safe. Telling a parent that you are gay, coming forward with a mistake, or opening up about a struggle with your mental health is less likely to happen if there is no perceived safety. The judgement of "What will they think about me?" is often the scariest part of opening up to someone. These conversations are more likely to happen if the person listening *withholds judgement*. This means that we don't offer our own thoughts or opinions, *unless it is asked for*. Again, "first seek to understand, then to be understood".

Many people who struggle with their mental health don't tell anyone. Quality relationships, fuelled by quality conversations, can provide the space for people to open up. At the very least, you may find out that your Dad once did a "runner".

I met Ernie for the first time after a talk I gave about work-life balance. We decided to meet for a coffee and go for a walk. It was the first time we had a proper conversation. We took a deep interest in each other's lives.

We talked about faith, our biggest dreams, our partners, our upbringing, and were left with a mutual admiration for each other's work and, more importantly, each other as human beings. I have people I have known for decades who don't know about some of the things I spoke about with Ernie. Upon reflection, it was fuelled by great questions.

The next time we met, it was on my "home turf" at the nursing home where I work once a week. Again, we had a coffee and went for a walk. Ernie is a man of deep faith, and just before I had met with him that day, I had seen one of my favourite nursing home residents, who I will call Agnes.

Agnes also shared a deep faith and was approaching the end of her life. I asked Agnes, "What do you need from me?" "Pray for me," she said. I am not religious, but I love my patients. I tried my best and prayed. That day when I met with Ernie, I asked him whether he could pray for her. He offered me one better. "Can I meet her?" he asked.

I introduced Ernie to Agnes and her family, who were bedside. They ended up all praying together. Agnes and the family were incredibly grateful. A few days later, Agnes passed. I was appreciative of Ernie's willingness to serve in that moment, and Ernie was appreciative of the opportunity to do so.

I had only met Ernie twice, and he was rapidly becoming a good friend. This is the power of quality conversations. Often these need to happen organically, but you can increase your chances by asking questions, listening deeply, and being vulnerable.

Quality time is a multiplier

Quality time is when you are offering your undivided attention to the people you are with. Quantity of time is the how long you spend with someone and how long you have known them for. When it comes to deep and meaningful relationships, *quality trumps quantity*. Quantity alone doesn't guarantee anything. You could know someone for decades and still not have a close relationship with them. However, quality *and* quantity can be transformative to a relationship. These represent the people you can call in the middle of the night and who, one day, will attend your funeral and console your loved ones.

Quality time is about undivided attention.

Most people these days are time-poor and their attention is scattered across the various balls of life they are required to juggle. Therefore, giving your time and attention to someone sends a very strong signal — that they matter.

In May 2022, my incredible mother-in-law was diagnosed with advanced fallopian tube cancer. From this day onwards, I became her doctor because no-one was going to give her the level of attention that I was going to. I went to appointments with her, explained treatment options to her, sped up treatment when there were obstacles, and helped her and the family make big decisions.

Although I had known her for well over a decade, as I married her equally amazing daughter, we became much closer after she was diagnosed with cancer. We attended all her medically related appointments together and in the downtime, we would talk about family, friends, life's adversities, the futility of various conflicts in the family and, of course, Sri Lankan teledramas.

Over a relatively short period of time, I was upgraded from son-in-law to son. She would speak with pride that, "Gihan is not like a son-in-law, he's like a son". I would say similar things about her. "She's my second mother. I have been blessed with two amazing mothers." We have spent hours of quality time together. My mother-in-law knows one thing for sure, she matters to me.

The *Emperor's Three Questions* by the famous Russian writer Leo Tolstoy is a parable that eloquently encapsulates what it means to have quality time with someone else. The emperor offered the following three questions to his whole kingdom.

1. What is the best time to do each thing?
2. Who are the most important people to work with?
3. What is the most important thing to do at all times?

The emperor decided that if he only knew the answers to these questions, he would never stray in any matter. Whoever could answer the questions was promised a handsome reward. He received many responses but none met his satisfaction. His enquiry led him to the mountains to meet with a hermit who was said to be enlightened. The student was ready, so the teacher appeared. The hermit provided the insight he was looking for.

"Remember that there is only one important time and that is now. The present moment is the only time over which we have dominion. The most important person is always the person you are with, who is right before you, for who knows if you will have dealings with any other person in the future. The most important thing is to make the person standing at your side happy, for that alone is the pursuit of life."

Can you believe that this was written in 1903? It was true then. It is true now.

> *Quality time requires that you are present, make the person you are with the most important person in your life in that moment, and that you endeavour to make them happier.*

I want to point out a significant nuance to this parable. When you find yourself alone, you are still with someone. *Yourself.* When you are by yourself, *you* become the most important person and someone who is worthy of happiness. Ultimately, the most important relationship you will cultivate in your life is with the incredible human you see in the mirror.

Dr G's prescription

A happy life is built with quality relationships.

Turn to the corresponding page of your *Do Happy Workbook*, to complete the following exercise.

1. **Write down five people in your life that you want to cultivate a deeper relationship with.**

2. **Create opportunities with these people to have quality conversations and spend quality time with them.** For example, organise a coffee session, invite them to your house, or to a hike in the mountains.

3. **Design a MAM. What is a Minimum Absolute Must you can commit to on a daily basis that will strengthen your relationships? For example,**
   o Send a text of gratitude to someone you care about every day.

4. **Perform a 3650 forecast.**
   o 3650 X [Sending a gratitude text every day] = 3650 gratitude texts after 10 years. Remember, when you send a text, you will probably get a response. Bring on the quality relationships!

It may not always make sense to do this daily. For example, you don't necessarily need to talk to your best friend every day. It's possible they won't want that either. Regardless, the goal is consistency over a long time. Remember, relationships are a big rock — make them a priority and ensure that your calendar devotes time to people.

Chapter 8

Nature

*"Look deep into nature, and then you
will understand everything better."*
~ Albert Einstein

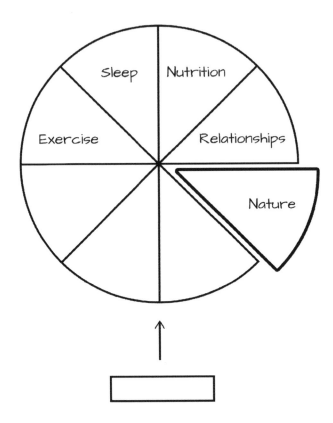

Richard Louv coined the term "Nature-Deficit Disorder". It's not an official medical term but intuitively, you know what he means. As humans have evolved socially and technologically, there has been an increasing shift to move indoors. Sure, we may have the occasional indoor plant but it's just not the same. We have become increasingly disconnected from nature. It is a significant, yet insidious, problem that is making people unhappy.

As the population grows, open spaces decrease, with land being developed for construction. When the land is exhausted, developments shift "upwards", resulting in apartment blocks and multi-story houses. Louv suggests that increasing evidence is linking nature-deficit disorder to diminished sensory experiences, attention difficulties, obesity, and higher rates of emotional and physical illnesses.

I spent a few years working in hospitals. I would leave home before sunrise, work indoors under artificial lighting all day, and return home after dark. During this time, maintaining my mental health was significantly harder. I loved utilising my medical knowledge, helping patients, and working with my inspiring colleagues, but I hated the lifestyle. I had invested over a decade of my life to become a doctor and I wasn't enjoying it. I was lost. I needed some time to think. In the gap between finishing a short-lived career in the hospitals and starting my training to become a General Practitioner (GP), I took six months off.

In my mid-20s, newly married and unsure about my future, we lucked out when my wife got a temporary job in Hobart, Australia. We moved there and had the time of our lives. My wife worked whilst I experienced retired life. I took guitar lessons and became mildly awesome at playing the chords to Adele songs. I took Judo lessons and got thrown so hard that I learnt how hard the earth was. I also wrote a blog that no-one read.

When my wife wasn't working, we explored Hobart together. We spent hours *outside*. In Hobart, wherever you go, you're surrounded by mountains, water bodies, or both — think waterfalls nestled in forests. We were fully immersed in nature. Even on a walk to the local supermarket, we could often see the iconic Mount Wellington, sometimes with snow on its peak. Our physical and mentally wellbeing was through the roof.

Increased exposure to nature has been shown to reduce symptoms of depression and stress and improve quality of life and mood. This could be due to multiple factors. Over time, we have evolved predominantly outdoors so it is likely that nature *is* our natural habitat. Nature encourages exploration and novelty of experience, creating a break from typical indoor routines. It also promotes physical activity, the importance of which we have already discussed in the *Exercise* section.

Nevertheless, the rise of digital technology has driven us to be largely indoor creatures. Convenience is hard to resist.

» Why walk when we can drive?
» Why play outside when you can binge on-demand streaming services?
» Why grow food in the garden when you can buy it and get it delivered to your house?
» Why look up at the sky when you can look down at your phone?

It may not always be the convenient option and it will require your most strained resource — time — but make no mistake about it, part of the happiness game is won *outside*.

The happiness game is won outside.

Embrace green and blue spaces

Green spaces refer to areas that are covered with grass, trees, or other vegetation. These spaces can include parks, gardens, forests, and other natural landscapes.

Blue spaces refer to areas that are dominated by water features, such as rivers, lakes, ponds, oceans, fountains and canals.

Many people slowly build a resistance to the busyness of city life and consider either a "tree change", i.e. moving inland to live in an area by the mountains, or a "sea change", i.e. moving to a more relaxed coastal area. Both have its appeals but you don't have to move away from the city to experience these green and blue spaces, just start by going *outside*.

In writing this book, my editor Lexi Wight reviewed this chapter and told me that "1000 hours outside" changed her life. I was intrigued so I investigated. The premise is simple — *commit to trying to spend 1000 hours outside in a 365-day period*. That's nearly *three hours a day*. My first reaction was probably the same as yours, "who has time for that?"

To spend 1,000 hours outside, we would need to completely change how we live our lives. Maybe that's the point. The 1000 hours outside movement was started by Ginny Yurich, a wife and mother of five, who wanted to help children reclaim their childhood and reconnect families. Ginny informs us that "the average child spends 4-7 hours a day on screens, but only gets 4-7 minutes of unstructured free play outside each day." Whether you are a child or not, we can all relate to these words. Something really significant has been lost over last few decades. Is it time to reclaim it?

If three hours a day seems like a stretch, I have good news. There are studies that suggest only *10-20 minutes* of exposure to the outdoors is the minimum time required to provide a benefit to your mental health. If your time in nature *exceeds two hours a week*, further research shows the impact to your wellbeing "increases significantly".

Pro tip:

If you're like most people, you might have some "uncomfortable" months — whether it's the cold and rain of winter or the sweltering heat of summer. Nature doesn't take any days off, so finding a way to get outside even on these less-than-ideal days can help you enjoy nature every day of the year. Remember, design for worst-case scenarios.

Get outside

In an ideal world, you would spend nearly three hours every day outside in nature. This would make you ridiculously happier. For most of us, at least at the start, it's not feasible. Practically speaking, until you truly see it as a *big rock*, why would you spend this long outside? To get some runs on the board, we need to focus on time and energy efficient strategies. I have just that.

Do what you already do inside, outside.

When I present this as an option to individuals or workplaces, I can often see a light bulb go off. We already have plenty of things that we do — eat, attend meetings, work, study, scroll on social media, or exercise. Just do it outside instead.

» Have your lunch outside.
» Ask your team if they would like to host the daily meeting outside.
» Exercise outside.
» Even if you are on your phone, why not do it outside?

> A few years ago, I had the pleasure of visiting Mirissa, a small town on the southern coast of Sri Lanka. It is known for its beaches, as well as whale watching. When you go on a boat and someone sees a whale, they yell "Tail up!", referring to the whale's tail, which is the last part to disappear back into the ocean.

Mirissa was the definition of a "blue space". I also got to do something I would normally do inside, outside. The resort we stayed at had an outdoor shower. Although privacy was not guaranteed, it was a special treat to shower outside.

You might not always have the luxury of showering outside by the beach, but I hope this story inspires you to think creatively and consider visiting Sri Lanka as well.

Dr G's prescription

Nature is defined as "all the animals, plants, and other things in the world that are not made by people, and all the events and processes that are not caused by people". Enjoy it. It is breath-taking and has immense benefits for our wellbeing and happiness. Let's aim for at least *10 minutes outside every day*.

Turn to the corresponding page of your *Do Happy Workbook*, and complete the following exercise:

1. **Generate a list of ideas to help you spend more time outside. The easiest way is to make a list of what you are already doing inside, and do it outside.**
   - Suggest walking meetings. A gamechanger if you have a lot of meetings.
   - Have your meals outside.
   - Read outside.
   - Do phone calls outside.

o Exercise outside.

o Study outside.

Alternatively, make time in nature a lifestyle.

o Join an outdoor sports group.

o Go for hikes on the weekends.

o Build a vegetable garden and keep it alive.

o Go camping.

o Volunteer with local organisations to help build or maintain nature trails.

2. **Design a MAM. For example,**

o Once you make breakfast, take it outside and sit on the porch.

o If you are meeting with someone, ask them if they want to do a walking catch up.

As the MAM becomes consistent on a daily basis, you can slowly do more. For example, after sitting down outside with your breakfast, actually eat it. After that, perhaps you can have all your meals outside.

3. **Perform a 3650 forecast.**

o 3650 X [10 minutes a day outside] = 36,500 minutes (608.3 hours) in nature over 10 years

4. **Consider doing the 1000 hour challenge.** At the time of writing, although I have never tried it, I am excited about the giving it a go.

Chapter 9

Kindness

"If you have to choose between being kind and being right,
choose being kind and you will always be right."

~ Unknown

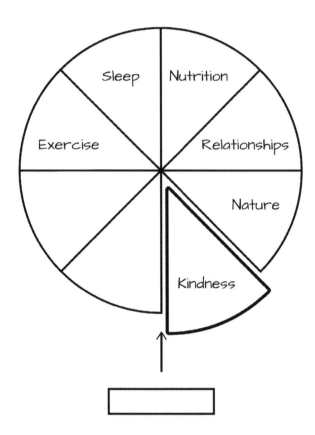

I get excited when I see an old lady struggle with their groceries. Here is why.

A group of foreign journalists were travelling with the Dalai Lama as he visited poverty-stricken village after village. In every village the locals would come out and present the Dalai Lama with gifts: a handful of rice, an old book — whatever they had. One of the journalists became angrier and angrier as he saw people who had practically nothing gifting what little they had and the Dalai Lama graciously accepting every offering.

In the final village of the tour, an old lady who lived under a tree was in tears because she had nothing to give the Dalai Lama except the clothes she was wearing. Then she started digging furiously at the foot of the tree and carefully unearthed an old, fraying, dirt-ridden dress; her wedding dress from many years ago. With tears still pouring down her wrinkled cheeks, she presented this to the Dalai Lama. He gracefully clasped his hands together and bowed humbly while accepting this gift.

This was the final straw for the journalist. He exploded with rage and challenged the Dalai Lama: *"Why on earth would you take a wedding dress from this poor lady?"*

The Dalai Lama replied: *"I accept the dress and the gifts not because I need them, but because my people need to give them."*

The old lady that struggles with their groceries may not always need my help. It may be me that needs to help her.

Kindness is the act of doing something that makes someone else's life better. BJ Fogg, the author of the New York Times Bestseller *Tiny Habits*, explains that behaviour is more likely to be repeated when it feels good before, during, or immediately after the act. Kindness usually feels great before, during, immediately after and sometimes long after the act itself. Kindness makes us feel good, which encourages us to be kind again.

*Kindness is the act of doing something that
make's someone else's life better.*

Whether it is listening to a friend who is struggling, donating to a charity
or helping an old lady with their groceries, you have likely experienced the
happiness inducing benefits of kindness. If you want to be happy all the
time, be kind. The research supports the phenomenon that behaviours
aimed to benefit someone else has an immense positive impact on
happiness. An interesting study published in the Journal of Positive
Psychology researched 788 participants who played and won money in a
game. They were given the choice to either keep the money or donate it.
The results showed that the people who donated money were subjectively
happier than people who kept money for themselves. Research has also
shown that in older adults, volunteering can be associated with better
psychological well-being and even delayed mortality.

Kindness seems to influence happiness at a chemical level. There
are strong links between kindness and "feel good" neurotransmitters
such as oxytocin, serotonin, and dopamine. Oxytocin, or the "love
hormone", is associated with connectedness and promotes positive
social interactions. Serotonin, the "feel good" neurotransmitter,
promotes feelings of happiness and wellbeing. Selective serotonin
reuptake inhibitors, or SSRIs, are a type of anti-depressant that works
by increasing serotonin levels in the brain. Dopamine is the "reward"
neurotransmitter that plays a key role in motivation, pleasure, and
reinforcing behaviour. The links between kindness and elevated levels
of these neurotransmitters explain the "helper's high" that people
experience when they help someone else.

The risk of being selfish

Life is hard. If it wasn't, you wouldn't need this book.

Sometimes we make it hard by taking on more hours at work or neglecting our self-care. Sometimes we actively chase things that are hard, like starting a business or having kids. Sometimes it's just hard, like losing a loved one.

Problems are many: traffic, climate change, parking fines, work-related stress, conflicts with family members, health issues, or sometimes debilitating depression and suicidal thoughts. When life is hard and we are faced with problems, we can become selfish. This is especially true if one of these problems is that you are unhappy. When we become absorbed in solving our own problems, *we forget that everyone else has problems too.*

> *Problems can make us selfish. The solution may not be to focus on our own problems but, rather, to help someone else with theirs.*

If in doubt, just be more like Grace.

> Grace was a 96-year-old nursing home resident that I looked after. She had endured the World Wars, the Great Depression, could barely walk, and had outlived all of her siblings and even one of her children. When I first entered her room, I noticed a pile of baby clothes that she had knitted.

"Who are these for Grace?" I asked.

"They are for the cute little premature babies at the hospital. Me and a couple of girlfriends have been knitting clothes for the hospital for decades now."

What an inspiring act of kindness that she has been able to sustain over *decades*. And you know what? Despite all her problems, Grace was happy. Grace decided that instead of focusing on her own problems, she would help someone else with theirs.

The three levels of kindness

The "hardness" of life allows kindness to exist. Kindness can occur at three scales.

1. Small scale kindness
2. Medium scale kindness
3. Large scale kindness

Despite the level of effort, time, and resources increasing as you progress from small scales of kindness to medium or large ones, each brings significant levels of happiness. All levels of kindness certainly bring a fullness, richness, and meaning to one's life.

Small scale kindness

These acts of kindness are easy, quick, and cheap. The aim is simple: try to make the person you are interacting with leave the interaction slightly better off than when they started.

Here are some examples:
- Making someone laugh with a Dad joke like, "Did you hear what happened to the movie about constipation?" [Pause for dramatic effect] "It hasn't come out yet." [Pause for hysterical laughter].
- Holding the door open for a stranger.
- Smiling at someone.
- Helping an old lady with their groceries.
- Writing a thank you note to someone you care about.
- Putting a few extra dollars in someone else's parking metre.
- Thanking a firefighter for running towards fire whilst anyone sane would run away.
- Sending a message of gratitude to a friend.

Medium scale kindness

This level of kindness requires more thought, effort, and resources. Often a medium scale act of kindness either serves a lot of people or it helps a handful of people in a profound way.

Here are some examples:

- Organising a charity event for a cause you feel strongly about.
- Volunteering to help disadvantaged people get into the workforce.
- Flying interstate to visit a sick loved one.
- Donating blood.
- Mentoring troubled youth.

Large scale kindness

- This level of kindness requires a lot of thought, effort, and resources. The impact of large-scale kindness can be measured by its breadth (i.e. how many people you help) or its depth (i.e. how deeply you help one or a few people).

Breadth

- Donate $1,000,000 to a worthy charity or social enterprise.
- Start a not-for-profit organisation.
- Start a movement and champion change for a prominent social problem.
- Build a business that creates jobs and reaches thousands of people.

Depth

- Adopt a child.
- Help someone overcome their addition to drugs.
- Save someone's life.

Overdoing kindness

You are on a plane and there is an emergency. The oxygen masks come down. Whose mask do you put on first? Your own. Always. It doesn't matter if your child is sitting next to you, you still put yours on first. *The order never changes.*

It is the same order for your own happiness.

Most people wake up, spend the whole day putting on oxygen masks for other people, and then they go to sleep.

These "other people" come in many forms depending on the roles you play in life:
- For a parent, their children.
- For a teacher, their students.
- For a doctor or a nurse, their patients.
- For an employee, their boss.
- For a business owner, their customers.
- For anyone, their family and friends.

This behaviour is usually rooted in trying to make other people's lives better. In other words, kindness. However, it's possible to overdo it, or, at least, do it in the wrong order. I have witnessed countless times that people who are admirably kind often do so at the expense of their own wellbeing. Eventually, something has to give.

A few years ago, I had the opportunity to create a wellbeing program for primary school kids. Pete was one of the primary school teachers I worked closely with. He was a great teacher and human being. He clearly loved the kids and did everything in his power to help them. At the end of the year, we had this conversation.

"I'm leaving."

"Why?!" I asked.

"It's too much. I am burnt out and I have nothing more to give. I need to look after myself. I can't sustain this."

"Do you have a job lined up? Which school are you moving to?"

"I am not just leaving the school. I am leaving the profession."

Pete put other people's oxygen mask on before his own. Eventually, he ran out of oxygen and he had to make a dramatic change. The education system lost a great teacher that day.

If you are someone who does a lot of good for the world, please don't stop. The world needs more people like you. However, if you are concerned that you are overdoing kindness, take that kindness and turn it inward. And do it *first*.

You put your oxygen mask on first so that you can help other people. You become useless if you run out of oxygen.

It's not: put yourself first, at the expense of others.
It's: put yourself first, then others.

What can putting your oxygen mask on first look like?

- Meditating for 20 minutes in the morning before checking your messages.
- Exercising after work before you return home to the inertia of being married with kids.
- Making time to call your best mate before you make other plans.
- Sitting outside in nature doing absolutely nothing before paying your bills.

Use the mindset of "first" to guide your actions throughout the day. Putting other people's oxygen masks may seem noble but, on its own, it is short-sighted. If you get the order right and put yourself first, it is sustainable.

Dr G's prescription

The world's problems provide an opportunity for us to be kind and, therefore, be happier.

Turn to the corresponding page of your *Do Happy Workbook*, to complete the following exercise.

1. **Write down 5-10 small acts of kindness that you can think of.**

2. **In the next 24 hours, aim to do 3 small acts of kindness.** It can be as simple as sending a message of gratitude to a friend, or offering a huge smile to the next person you see.

3. **Consider whether it's feasible to perform a medium or even large act of kindness in the next 12 months.** If it is, make a plan and work towards it. Good luck!

4. **Design a MAM. For example,**
    o   When someone asks you, "How are you?" respond with "Living the dream!" This will surely put a smile on their face and your own.
    o   Send a message to a friend and complete this sentence, "Hey! I was thinking of you and just want to thank you for [insert reason]." Press send.

As the MAM becomes consistent on a daily basis, you can slowly do more. Get creative and have fun with it.

5. **Perform a 3650 forecast:**
    o   3650 X [1 message of gratitude every day] = 3650 messages of gratitude after 10 years

Chapter 10

Gratitude

"Gratitude is the secret behind his smile."

~ Dr G's wife

Gratitude helped Owen turn a breakup into a breakthrough.

She was "the one". After nearly two years together, she broke up with Owen.

He had pictured a whole life with her — buying a house, having kids, and fostering a few fur babies. Then, out of the blue, she told him that it was over. Owen's world came crashing down. He started to see the world as if it was a bad place full of bad people.

Pessimism became his default state. Everything in his life seemed dark. It was like he was seeing the world through black-tinted glasses.

When Owen came to see me, the first thing we started was a gratitude journaling practice. I asked him to write at least two things he was grateful for every day. The first thing had to be about himself. The second thing could be about someone or something else. He was sceptical but he obliged. After a few weeks,

"I got into a car crash," Owen said.

"Jeez!"

"It was weird."

"Why?"

"I wasn't annoyed or angry or frustrated."

"What do you mean?"

"I was already struggling since I broke up with Jemma. Getting rear-ended by that guy should have been my final confirmation that everything is falling apart."

"It wasn't?"

"My mind raced straight to gratitude!"

"Explain."

"I was grateful that no-one was hurt. I was grateful that my insurance would cover the repairs. I was even grateful that I was grateful! I think I am starting to see the world differently."

When life becomes difficult, it can be easy to see all of life as that difficulty. Gratitude helps us to see the bigger picture.

When life becomes difficult, it can be easy to
see all of life as that difficulty.

Research by Robert A. Emmons and Michael McCullough highlights the significant benefits of gratitude journaling, showing that in as little as 21 days, we can develop a more positive and optimistic outlook on life. Cultivating gratitude helps to foster feelings of being loved and cared for, strengthen social bonds, inspire kindness to and from others, and allows us to cope better with stress.

Barbara's Fredrickson's work suggests that gratitude also expands our "thought-action repertoire", referring to our capacity to generate a wider range of thoughts and behaviours that can be used to respond to life and its circumstances. In other words, gratitude makes us more psychologically and physically resourceful, thereby enhancing our ability to *Do Happy*.

Gratitude makes us more psychologically
and physically resourceful.

Gratitude and stegosaurus clouds

The most elegant description of depression and anxiety I have heard is by a monk named Ajahn Brahm.

Feeling sad or depressed comes from having negative thoughts about what has already happened in the past.

Feeling worried or anxious comes from having negative thoughts about what may happen in the future.

Dwelling on the past or worrying about the future is a recipe for unhappiness. A logical solution is to cultivate a practice that allows you to have positive thoughts about what has happened in the past, what may happen in the future, and what is happening now. *This is gratitude.* A profound, yet less obvious next step is to cultivate internal silence and have less thoughts altogether. A quieter mind is a happier mind. See Figure 9.

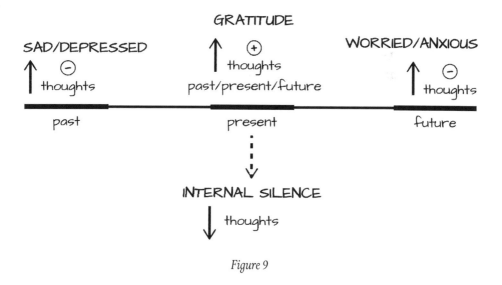

Figure 9

It's a lot like the sun and the clouds. The sun is *always* there. Whether it's cloudy or night time, the sun is always present and shining bright. Clouds can get in the way and make us lose sight of the sun. The sun represents the default state of happiness that we always have access to — a state of peace, contentment, and fulfilment that carries a lot of depth and wisdom. Although it is hard to explain in words, it can be experienced by us all. It is very different to the transient and fleeting feeling of happiness.

Our default state is happiness.

The clouds represent our thoughts and feelings. They obstruct the sun. When we are thinking and feeling depressed or anxious, it's like having a lot of dark, thick clouds obstructing the sun. Sometimes these clouds can turn into thunderstorms.

Gratitude allows us to have more helpful and positive thoughts. Instead of thunderstorms, perhaps these clouds look like a cool stegosaurus. However, although they look cool, the stegosaurus clouds are still clouds. They still obstruct the sun. They just look better. Nevertheless, the skill of cultivating stegosaurus clouds, formally known as practising gratitude, will lead to an extraordinary experience of life. Before I show you how, I have to mention the next step.

If gratitude helps us see stegosaurus clouds, meditation allows us to have fewer clouds or, in other words, fewer thoughts. A quieter or even silent mind, means you can directly experience the nature of the "sun". For me, experiencing the sun has confirmed that our default state is one of happiness. It is simply our thoughts and feelings that cloud it. There are 3 chapters on *Meditation* in this book, each written to progressively help you experience this for yourself. Until then, let's delve into gratitude and stegosaurus clouds.

Gratitude helps us see the stegosaurus clouds. Meditation helps us have less clouds, so we can directly experience the sun.

How to practise gratitude

The first step is simple: get an empty journal. Without something to write in, there is no gratitude practice. Once you have the journal, it's time to cultivate some stegosaurus clouds.

The rules

The following four rules will revolutionise your gratitude practice:

- a. Write it down.
- b. Make it specific.
- c. Make it different each time.
- d. Do it every day.

Write it down

Ignore the temptation to "just think about it" in your head. There are two reasons you should write it down. Firstly, it forces you to clarify exactly what you are grateful for. Secondly, with regular journaling, you will have books full of things you are grateful for. It is incredible to be able to flick through the pages and remind yourself of all the things that have made you grateful over the last few days, weeks, months, or years. If it made you happy once, it can make you happy over and over again.

What do you write?

1. Something about yourself (compulsory)

Most people struggle with writing something they are grateful for about themselves. We live in a society where we are expected to be "humble" and this is misconstrued as having to downplay ourselves. Over time, this can crush one's self worth, self-esteem and self-confidence. All the self's! This part of the practice is the only thing I consider *compulsory*. It is not a muscle that is often flexed. We are all worthy. We all have value. We all have an "inner awesomeness". Regularly writing something about yourself helps you discover it. After doing this for many years, I believe that it is this practice that has made my sense of self-worth *undeniable*. My friend, I want the same for you.

I am grateful that I held the door open for the elderly lady that was trying to negotiate opening the door and holding on to her walker for balance. This shows that I am kind and considerate.

I am grateful that I visited my friend at the hospital. I was busy but I made the time. This shows that I am caring and prioritise what's important.

2. Something about someone else

If we all have an inner awesomeness within us, that means everyone else does too. I usually write about my wife and then tell her about it. It has strengthened our marriage beyond measure. Alternatively, I pick someone else in my life (e.g. parents, family, friends, strangers, work colleagues) and write about them. If it's feasible, I make an effort to tell them about it because it helps others to see the stegosaurus clouds as well.

I am grateful that my wife packed me lunch for work because I went to sleep early and forgot. I would eventually starve to death without her.

> I am grateful that my Mum still tells me to lock my doors when I am driving. She is cute. She will never stop caring about me.

3. Something you take for granted

Life is a concoction of beautiful things that we take for granted. If we are breathing and still alive, no matter the circumstances, every single person can have something that they're grateful for.

> I love the fact that even if I have a bad day, the sun goes down and comes up the next day and I have another shot at it!

> I saw a possum with a baby possum on its back running across the top of my fence yesterday. It was strangely epic.

> I saw a monkey breastfeeding at a monkey forest in Bali. It was something I didn't know I needed to see, until I saw it.

4. Something about work/study

In a 168-hour week, we could spend more than 40 hours working or studying. If we don't find meaning and fulfilment from the thing that we spend a quarter of our adult life doing, it is a problem. A daily gratitude practice will allow you to be thankful for the work you do, what you learn through your studies, the money you earn, the people you meet along the way, and the impact you have.

I got paid today. I am grateful to our finances manager for going through my timesheet and ensuring the right amount of money hit my account. I can now proceed to feed myself and my family.

Every time I walk into my office, the heater has already been turned on. I am blessed to work with people who are so considerate.

I am loving my university degree. I met Jenny in my first class and we immediately hit it off. I am looking forward to seeing where this friendship goes.

5. Something about difficult circumstances

Life is hard. However, every dark cloud has a silver lining. There can be beauty in adversity. Find it and then write about it.

> Maintaining a long-distance relationship for 6 years earned me the privilege of marrying my best friend (true story).

> Getting bullied at school made me more compassionate and empathetic. If I wasn't bullied, *Do Happy* would never have been born.

> My legendary mother-in-law getting diagnosed with cancer led us to spend a lot more time together. Our relationship has deepened beyond measure.

6. Something about difficult people

No one is fundamentally annoying. They can just do things that are annoying. If you can cultivate gratitude towards them, it dissipates unhelpful emotions and thoughts, such as anger and frustration, and replaces it with compassion, kindness, and generosity.

*"Holding on to anger is like grasping a hot coal
with the intent of throwing it at someone else;
you are the one who gets burned."*
~ Buddha

John told my friends that I can't be trusted. This is an opportunity to slow down, avoid any impulsive reactions, and better understand the situation before responding. This will make me more patient and calmer under stress.

Mary called me "weak and soft". I responded by saying, "Don't mistake my kindness for weakness." I am grateful that I was able to stand up for myself with class.

Neha pushed my buttons to the point where I simply burst out in anger. I said some regretful things. I am grateful to have learnt the capacity of anger to cause more harm. I need to be more careful when I am angry.

Make it specific

Specificity can be the difference between a practice that fizzles out and one that lasts a lifetime. Usually, people fall into the trap of staying too general. For example, writing "I am grateful for my wife's support... my health... my family... my friends... my well-paying job" are all too general.

On the other hand, being specific allows for two things. Firstly, it cultivates gratitude more effectively. Writing, "I am grateful for my wife for carving out two hours yesterday to allow me to write my '*Do Happy*' book. She is an absolute legend." is much better than "I am grateful for my wife's support." Secondly, specificity allows for you to make it different (see below).

Make it different

Whatever you write, it has to be *different every single day for the rest of your life*. You can't write the same thing twice. You may be asking, is that possible? Not only is it possible, it is a game changer.

This is the common trend (See *Figure 10*) I see with people who have a gratitude practice that fizzles out. At the start, it's hard to write things to be grateful for because it's a muscle people are not used to flexing. After a while, people build some momentum. Then, they run out of things to write. They plateau. So, what do most people do? They stop. It's a tragedy because it is at this point that the potential for magic begins. I call this point the "turning point". Once you run out of the obvious things to be grateful for, you start to look outside your immediate circumstances. You literally start *scanning the world for gratitude*. It's like getting a new set of prescription glasses because you will start to see the world through a lens of gratitude.

You will find a reason to be grateful in *everything*. It could be your partner shaking their head after you make a terrible joke or even noticing the intricate details of a leaf (seriously, look at a leaf really closely and you will realise how beautiful it is!). And of course, it could be seeing a possum with its baby on their back crawl across your fence.

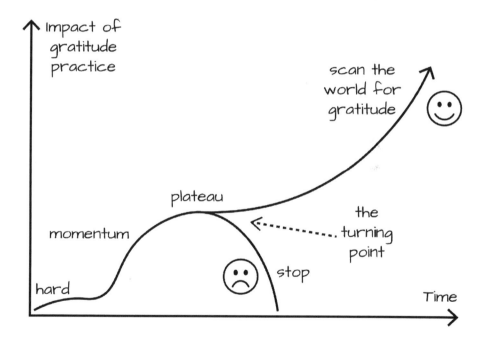

Figure 10

How do you make it different every day? *Permutations.*

Permutations refer to the different ways you can arrange a set of variables. Let me show you how to use permutations to generate an *infinite* number of things to be grateful for. When it comes to gratitude, there are five variables that can be arranged (See Figure 11).

1. *Time:* Past, Present, Future
2. *Event:* What happened (past), is happening (present), or will happen (future)?
3. *Thought:* What was the line of thinking involved?
4. *Action:* What was the line of action/inaction involved?
5. *Character:* What does this show about me?

Figure 11

Due to the nature of permutations, changing even one of the above five variables will generate a completely new thing to be grateful for. Understanding the power of permutations will allow you to *write something different every day for the rest of your life.*

> **Change any variable and you will have**
> **something new you can be grateful for.**

1. **Pick the time (past, present, or future):** Past
2. **What happened?** I played tennis ball cricket with my best mates from school. I scored the winning runs.
3. **What was the line of thinking involved?** I love the challenge and rush of a heroic batting innings that goes down to the wire.
4. **What was the line of action/inaction involved?** I calculated the runs required per over and accounted for the weaker bowlers I knew I could hit for 6!
5. **What does this show about me?** I thrive under pressure.

This is what I would write.

"I played tennis ball cricket with my best mates from school. I scored the winning runs. I love the challenge and rush of a heroic batting innings that goes down to the wire. I calculated the runs required per over and accounted for the weaker bowlers I knew I could hit for 6! I thrive under pressure."

Notice that for the same example, if you change any of the variables, you generate a different thing to be grateful for.

1. **Pick the time (past, present or future):** Past
2. **What happened?** I played tennis ball cricket with my best mates from school. I scored the winning runs.
3. **What was the line of thinking involved?** I am creating memories with my friends that we will reminisce about in the future.
4. **What was the line of action/inaction involved?** I calculated the runs required per over and accounted for the weaker bowlers I knew I could hit for 6!
5. **What does this show about me?** I love creating meaningful moments with my best mates.

This is what I would write.

"I played tennis ball cricket with my best mates from school. I scored the winning runs. I am creating memories with my friends that we will reminisce about in the future. I calculated the runs require per over and accounted for the weaker bowlers I could hit for 6! I love creating meaningful moments with my best mates."

On the following page is another example.

1. **Pick the time (past, present or future):** Future.

2. **What will happen?** I will travel through Europe next year.

3. **What was the line of thinking involved?** I gave myself permission to take two months off from work.

4. **What was the line of action/inaction involved?** I saved $30,000 over the last 18 months to allow my family to have an incredible experience.

5. **What does this show about me?** I love to travel and experience new cultures and perspectives.

This is what I would write:

"I travelled through Europe. I gave myself permission to take 6 weeks off from work. I saved $30,000 over the last 18 months to allow my family to have an incredible experience. I love to travel and experience new cultures and perspectives."

Do it every day

The beauty of never repeating anything is that by the end of the year, you will have 365 specific and uniquely different reasons to be grateful for yourself, other people, and all of life's intricacies. Imagine what this will do for your self-esteem and self-confidence. Imagine what it would do for your relationships. If you apply the 3650 rule, after 10 years, it's 3650 specific and uniquely different things. This practice will transform your life, with noticeable results in just a few weeks.

Dr G's prescription

Gratitude is a superpower that will help you have positive thoughts about what has happened in the past, what may happen in the future, and what is happening now. If you haven't already, get a gratitude journal and start writing. Do it for the rest of your life.

Turn to the corresponding page of your *Do Happy Workbook*, to complete the following exercise.

1.   **Write one thing you are grateful for about:**
    a.   Yourself
    b.   Someone else
    c.   Something you take for granted
    d.   Work/study
    e.   A difficult circumstance
    f.   A difficult person

2.   **Design a MAM. For example,**
    o   Write *one* thing you are grateful for about yourself every day.

As the MAM becomes consistent on a daily basis, it will naturally grow.

3.   **Perform a 3650 forecast:**
    o   3650 X [Writing 1 specific and unique reason to be grateful for yourself every day] = 3650 reasons that confirm you are undeniably amazing after 10 years.

Chapter 11

Meditation for Focus

"The secret of health for both mind and body is not to mourn for the past, worry about the future, or anticipate troubles, but to live in the present moment wisely and earnestly."
~ Buddha

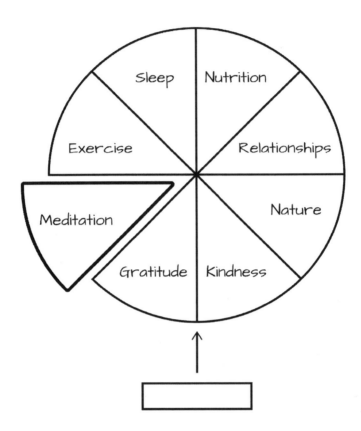

Kung-Fu Panda is the story of Po, a large, lazy, and clumsy panda who dreams of being a great martial artist. When Po starts his training with Master Shifu and the Furious Five, he quickly starts to believe that he is untrainable. Po meets with the Master Oogway and tells him how much he sucks and how the others don't think that he belongs. He thinks about quitting. Master Oogway, like any wise guru, calmly tells him that he is too concerned about the past and the future and then delivers one of my favourite quotes that any cartoon turtle has said,

"Yesterday is history, tomorrow is a mystery,
but today is a gift. That is why it's called the present."
~ Master Oogway (Kung-Fu Panda)

In the previous chapter on gratitude, I introduced the analogy of the sun and the clouds. The sun is always there. The sun represents a default state of happiness that transcends beyond our traditional understanding of happiness as a feeling that comes and goes. The clouds represent the thoughts that "obstruct" the sun. A wandering and busy mind is one that is "full of clouds", it is an unhappy mind.

Harvard psychologists Matthew A. Killingsworth and Daniel T. Gilbert conducted a study that confirmed this. The pair developed an app that contacted 2250 volunteers at random intervals during the day to ask how they are feeling, what they were doing, and whether they were thinking about their current activity or about something else that was pleasant, neutral, or unpleasant. They gathered 250,000 data points and found that "47% of waking hours is spent thinking about what isn't going on."

Our unique ability to think is what separates us from the animal kingdom. It also comes at a cost. Killingsworth and Gilbert suggest that "the ability to think about what is not happening is a cognitive achievement that comes at an emotional cost." The research suggests that "how often our minds leave the present and where it tends to go is a better predictor of happiness than the activities in which we are engaged". Often, we blame our busy lives for our unhappiness. Although a busy life is obvious, a busy mind is insidious. If you are unhappy, perhaps it's not what you are doing but rather your wandering mind and where it wanders to that needs to be addressed. This aligns with ancient philosophical and religious traditions that have emphasised the importance of being in the present moment for thousands of years.

A wandering mind is an unhappy mind.

Meditation can train your mind to *focus on one thing*. Using the sun and clouds analogy, it's like picking *one* cloud and focusing only on that. This helps your mind to build the muscle of staying still, instead of wandering. Just like lifting weights at the gym builds your physical muscles, meditation builds your "mental muscles". You practise noticing when your mind wanders and bringing it back to your object of focus (e.g. the breath). Much like building your physical strength helps you to lift heavy objects, regular meditation strengthens your mind's ability to lift the heavy "mental weights" of life's challenges and difficulties, leading to an overall sense of happiness.

What to focus on

There are hundreds of different meditation techniques and it can get overwhelming. Ultimately, all you need is an *object of focus*. It is this object that you bring your attention back to. The object can be *anything*.

5 common objects of focus

Although the object of focus can be anything, here are five commonly used options.

1.   5,4,3,2,1
2.   The breath
3.   Body scan
4.   Loving kindness
5.   Guided meditation

5,4,3,2,1

This strategy uses your 5 senses — sight, hearing, touch, smell, and taste — as your object of focus.

Bring your attention to:

- 5 things that you can *see*
- 4 things that you can *hear*
- 3 things that you can *feel*
- 2 things that you can *smell*
- 1 thing that you can *taste*

Focus on one thing at a time and gently move your awareness from one object to another. Your mind will wander, that's normal. When you realise it has wandered, simply bring it back to your object of focus. Developing an awareness of when your mind has wandered and bringing your attention back is the muscle you are trying to build. Keep in mind that the 5,4,3,2,1 numbers are arbitrary and can be changed to suit your needs. You can mix and match as you please. For example, some days you might observe 5 things for each of the senses. Be creative and have fun with it.

Developing an awareness of when your mind has wandered and
bringing your attention back is the muscle
you are trying to build.

The breath

The body breathes whether you are aware of it or not. The breath is always available to you (hopefully) which makes it a useful object of focus to anchor the mind and your awareness. If you notice your mind wandering, bring it back to your breath. You can observe your breath at multiple points — your lips, nostrils, chest, or abdomen.

A word of warning. It is possible that your mind, one that has been accustomed to think its whole life, will find watching the breath incredibly hard and boring. That's normal. If you persist, you may start to observe the "infinite beauty of the breath". Although this is a topic that is above my paygrade, I have experienced glimpses of it and I can confirm — it's beautiful.

Body scan

Our body is *always* present. It has no choice but to be exactly where it is. It is our mind that wanders elsewhere. Therefore, the body itself can become a useful and wise object of focus. Similar to the 5,4,3,2,1 method, you can start by bringing your awareness to your toes and slowly scan up your body, like a photocopier, until you reach your head. As you do this, notice any discomforts, sensations, or tensions in your body. As your mind wanders, and it will, just bring it back to the body part you are observing.

Loving kindness

In loving kindness meditation you focus on different beings, human or otherwise, and cultivate love and kindness towards them. When I first started doing this, it felt somewhat out there. However, it has become one of the most important practices in my life.

Start by closing your eyes and visualising someone for whom it is easy to direct positive energy towards. Try to visualise this person in as much detail as possible. It may be your child, your partner, your best friend, your mum, your dad, or a pet. Wish them well with a mantra like "I wish you nothing but the best. I wish you love and joy and freedom from pain and suffering." Aim to do this with the level of care and affection a parent would offer a child. Once you are ready, move onto someone else and wish them well with the same mantra. As your mind wanders, and it will, gently bring it back to the person you are focusing on.

Continue this practice, gradually extending love and kindness to your suburb, then your state and country, and eventually to the whole world. Once you have spread love and kindness towards every being in the world, there is one person left, *you*. Harness all of that love and kindness that you have cultivated and direct it inwards. Use the same mantra but this time, to yourself.

Love and kindness are powerful objects of focus. If you repeatedly practise directing them towards others and yourself, you will start to see everything through a lens of love, kindness, compassion, and understanding. The worlds need more of this.

Guided meditation

The object of focus in this setting becomes someone else's instructions. Find an app (e.g. Smiling Mind, Headspace), pick a guided meditation, and follow along. If you are just getting started, this is a great way to begin because you can find a guided meditations for all of the above types of meditation and more.

Dr G's prescription

A wandering mind is an unhappy mind. Meditation can be used to bring your attention to what is happening now by training your mind to focus on one thing.

Turn to the corresponding page of your *Do Happy Workbook*, to complete the following exercise.

1. **Choose one of the 5 objects of focus that you want to experiment with.**

2. **Design a MAM. For example,**
    o   Bring your attention to one thing you can see for 10 seconds (5,4,3,2,1 MAM).
    o   Take one mindful breath (Breath MAM).

- o Bring your attention to one part of your body for 10 seconds (Body scan MAM).
- o Visualise one person you care about and, in your mind, wish them all the best (Loving kindness MAM).
- o Open your meditation app, pick one track and listen to only the first minute (Guided meditation app).

3. **Perform a 3650 forecast:**
    - o 3650 X [Focus on one thing you can see for 10s every day] = 36,500 seconds (608.3 minutes/10.1 hours) of mindful moments over 10 years.
    - o 3650 X [1 mindful breath every day] = 3650 mindful breaths over 10 years.
    - o 3650 X [Focus on one body part for 10s every day] = 36,500 seconds (608.3 minutes/10.1 hours) of mindful moments over 10 years.
    - o 3650 X [Directing love and kindness to one person every day] = 3650 acts of love and kindness over 10 years.
    - o 3650 X [Listen to 1 minute of a guided meditation track every day] = 3650 minutes (60.8 hours) of meditation over 10 years.

Chapter 12
Replace Screen Time

"The reason we struggle with insecurity is because we compare our behind-the-scenes with everyone else's highlight reel."
~ Steve Furtick

The first ever smartphone, IBM Simon, was invented in 1992 by IBM. It had a touch screen, allowed you to send and receive emails, and included built-in programs like a calendar and address book. In 2007, Apple released the iPhone, irreversibly changing the world in the process. Although the power we have at our fingertips seems like something out of a science fiction movie, it can also make people unhappy.

Meet 23-year-old Shara.

"My self-esteem is really low. I feel terrible and down most of the time."

"How much time do you spend on screens?" (This is usually the biggest untapped opportunity for happiness in this age group so I went straight for it.)

"I don't know."

"Check."

She checks her screen time tracker on her phone.

"10 hours."

"A week?"

"No. A day. Most of it is on social media."

"How often do you check your phone?" I asked.

"Maybe every 5-10 minutes."

I started to lose what's left of my hair in real time.

"Is that a lot?"

"Delete all your social media apps for two weeks."

"What? Why? I can't do that."

"Do you want better self-esteem and to feel better?"

"Yes, of course."

"Then delete all your apps. If you do it for two weeks, we can see what happens to your mental health. I think it will improve. If you can't do it for two weeks, then we have a different problem."

"OK, I will try".

She sees me a week later.

"How did you go with deleting your social media apps?" I asked curiously.

"I did it for four days but then I had to reactivate one of my accounts."

"Why?"

"This guy I like invited me to a party. I dressed up and I went. We all got drunk. He passed out on the couch before 9pm. I didn't know anyone there and I was quite drunk as well."

"And then?"

"Well, I was crying and I needed to get out of there. I called a taxi. On the way home, I managed to stop crying so I opened one of my social media accounts. I fixed my hair, managed a smile and took a selfie and posted it."

Shara couldn't avoid social media apps for even two weeks. It's not her fault. The lure of the internet, designed to capture and keep our attention, is too strong for willpower alone.

Research suggests one thing clearly, although screen time can be beneficial, excessive and inappropriate use is harmful. In a Harvard Business Review article, authors Holly Shakya and Nicholas Christakis reviewed research findings that found the "use of social media may detract from face-to-face relationships, reduce investment in meaningful activities, increase sedentary behaviour by encouraging more screen time, lead to internet addiction, and erode self-esteem". The authors had also conducted their own study, finding that the more you use social media, "the worse you feel". It was evident that given people tend to display the most positive aspects of their lives on social media, self-comparison can lead one to believe that their own life compares inferiorly to that of others. Furthermore, the time we spend on screens and social interactions, steals from our ability to enjoy real-life experiences. Another study suggested that "digital device dependency, screen time induced poor sleep quality, and content influence negativity" is associated with "suicidal tendencies and symptoms of depression". Screen time is a serious problem.

The three major costs

There are three major costs of excessive and unnecessary screen time:
1. Opportunity cost
2. Attention switching cost
3. Mind cost

Note that when I say unnecessary screen time, I refer to non-educational and non-work/study related screen time.

Opportunity cost

Opportunity cost states that when you say "yes" to one thing, you are saying "no" to an infinite number of other things. Saying "yes" to unnecessary screen time may carry the biggest opportunity cost of our time.

When you say yes to screen time, what do you say no to?
- Being present with your family.
- Building a business.
- Exercising.
- Rest (physical and mental).
- Meeting someone new.
- Writing a book (guilty).
- Yoga.
- Playing with your kids.
- Your favourite hobby.
- A date with your partner.

When you say "yes" to one thing, you are saying
"no" to an infinite number of other things.

If someone is unhappy *and* they spend a lot of time on their screens, I get excited. The solution may be as simple as reducing the screen time and replacing it with the fundamentals of Doing Happy.

Attention switching cost

Screen time can be in the form of a binge (i.e. scrolling social media for 3 hours) or frequent intermittent snacking (i.e. checking your phone every 5 minutes). Screen time snacking has an immense cost.

Let's find out how costly it is. I learnt the following exercise from Dan Martell, a Canadian entrepreneur and author of *Buy Back Your Time*.

It is designed to demonstrate the inefficiency and ineffectiveness of switching between tasks. Not only does this affect productivity, it has significant happiness implications.

Put this book down and grab a stopwatch:

1. Recite the alphabet from A through to Z as fast as you can. Time yourself. How long did it take you? Write it down.
2. Recite the numbers from 1 through to 26 as fast as you can. Time yourself. How long did it take you?
3. Now alternate between 1 letter of the alphabet and 1 number until you get to the number 26. For example, A1 B2 C3 etc. Time yourself. How long did it take you?

Here are my results:
- Alphabet — 3.88 seconds
- Numbers — 6.44 seconds
- Alternating — 1 minute 10 seconds

If I just did the alphabet and then the numbers one after the other, it would have taken me 10.32 seconds (3.88 + 6.44). Alternating between the alphabet and numbers took me an *extra* 59.68 seconds.

This is the cost of attention switching. It causes mental and physical fatigue, reduces your performance, and stalls your productivity. Nothing about this is happiness-inducing. I have met people who literally check their phone every five minutes. I can't bear to calculate the attention switching cost and the resulting cost to their happiness.

Mind cost

The cost to the mind is the greatest cost of all. In the previous chapter, we learnt that a wandering mind is an unhappy mind. Excessive screen time, both as a binge and as intermittent frequent snacking, contributes in three main ways to a wandering mind.

Screen time can make your mind wander *more, faster,* and to *unhelpful places.*

More

You have more thoughts about more things. To use the sun and the clouds analogy from earlier, this means more clouds that obstruct the sun.

Faster

Your mind is not only wandering, it is racing. Sometimes referred to as the "monkey brain", thoughts jump from one to another at a rapid speed. It is not a pleasant experience.

Unhelpful places

Excessive screen time can significantly impact the quality of our thoughts, causing our mind to wander to "unhelpful places". The two most common places are a sense of *not enoughness* and *loneliness.*

Not enoughness

Our tendency to compare ourselves to others stems from our evolutionary history. Humans have always craved belonging, living in tribes where collaboration and strong bonds increased chances of survival through better safety, mating opportunities, and access to food. The members of the tribe who became isolated were at a higher risk of dying.

The ability to compare oneself to others helped tribe members gauge their standing within the group, prompting actions to improve their positioning when needed. In the online world, we can compare ourselves with an infinite number of "tribe members" on the internet, making it easy to feel inadequate and think we are "not enough".

> *"The reason we struggle with insecurity is because we compare our behind-the-scenes with everyone else's highlight reel."*
> **~ Steve Furtick**

Loneliness

Dunbar's number suggests that quality social connections in one's life is best at or under 150 people. You may have thousands of "friends" or "followers" online but would they come to your funeral?

The world we interact with online is vast and superficial. The world we interact with in the "real world" is narrow and has the potential for depth. An extreme way to demonstrate this is with your death.

If you die, what percentage of the people you interact regularly with online would mourn your death and attend your funeral? Probably a low percentage.

If you die, what percentage of the people you interact regularly with in the real world would mourn your death and attend your funeral? Probably a high percentage.

This is not to disparage the people we meet online. I have met some wonderful people through the power of social media and the internet. It is simply a way to understand the loneliness and lack of belonging that excessive screen time can lead to despite having a lot of "friends" online.

The 4 R's: Review, Remove or Reduce, Replace

Given the costs of unnecessary screen time to your life and wellbeing, I suggest implementing the 4 R's.

1. Review
2. Remove
3. Reduce
4. Replace

Review

Spend a week writing down *every time* you use a screen for a non-educational/work purpose. Document when you viewed a screen (e.g. phone, tablet, laptop, TV) and for how long. Whether you have just scrolled on YouTube for three hours or checked your phone for 10 seconds while you are in line for a coffee, write *everything* down.

This exercise will bring awareness to the quantity and frequency of your screen time habits. You are only building awareness here. We are not changing anything yet.

Remove

This is the simplest (not easiest) way to rapidly eliminate unnecessary screen time. *Removing* screen time will *immediately* free up time and energy that you can invest into actions that improve your happiness and progress your life goals.

It might seem impossible. For example, deleting a social media app might feel life threatening. All I can say is that if you are struggling with your mental health *and* you spend hours on screens every day, I strongly recommend you try it. Don't think of it as a forever thing. Think of it as a detox. Try it for a day or a week and see. If you say "No" to unnecessary screen time (e.g. delete a social media app off your phone), you have the ability to say "Yes" to a lot of things (see "Replace" on the next page).

Reduce

Alternatively, you can *reduce* your screen time usage. There are two main principles I advise when it comes to reducing screen time.

Firstly, batching. Batching involves stacking all your screen time into one block of scheduled time. If it's scheduled, it's intentional. If it's intentional, you want to do it and it's not a distraction. If it's stacked together, you eliminate "snacking" and its attention switching cost. My favourite way is with an app blocker which allows me to predetermine the times where I will allow myself to check an app or website. If I try to check outside of those times (and I do try!), I get a friendly message saying "Stop wasting your time. Go be productive!"

Secondly, decide what you are going to watch *before* you open up a screen. You will increase your chances of being intentional and viewing content that is beneficial to you. This will reduce the mind cost of screen time that often comes from mindless scrolling.

Replace

Once you review your screen time usage and then remove or reduce it, you are left with three incredibly powerful resources: time, energy, and attention. If you are interested in becoming happier, funnel these three resources into one or more of the fundamentals of Doing Happy. Instead of jumping on a screen, you could call someone you care about (relationships), send a message thanking someone for their friendship (gratitude), notice five things that you can see (meditation for focus), go for a run (exercise), go to bed one hour earlier (sleep), immerse yourself in the great outdoors (nature), or eat a fruit and enjoy it without distraction (nutrition).

If you are someone who spends hours engaging in unnecessary screen time, the 4 R's will give you your life back.

Could you be addicted?

Judson Brewer in his book, *The Craving Mind*, defines addiction as "continued use despite adverse consequences". We often associate addiction with alcohol and drugs because the adverse consequences with these types of addictions are obvious. We don't associate addiction with more socially acceptable vices such as screens. For many people, their screen use meets the definition of addiction.

According to the Transport Accident Commission (TAC), "drivers are 10 times more at risk of crashing if they are texting, browsing or emailing on their mobile phone". In the same breath, "one third of drivers admit to using their phone illegally while driving". Continued use (i.e. texting while driving) despite adverse consequences (i.e. increased crash risk). In other words, it's an addiction.

The evidence for the negative consequences of excessive screen time on your mental health is undeniable. If you want to remove or reduce screen time from your life but you find yourself unable to, you may be addicted. *There is no shame in this.* Your willpower is competing against billion-dollar giants who design their products to capture and keep your attention. If you are concerned, consider seeking professional help. I also highly recommend reading Judson Brewer's book, *The Craving Mind*.

Dr G's prescription

Excessive screen time is a serious problem. It can incur three major costs to your wellbeing: an opportunity cost, attention switching cost, and a cost to your mind.

Turn to the corresponding page of your *Do Happy Workbook*, to complete the following exercise.

1. **Do the 4 R's.**
   - *Review:* Use the table in the workbook and document your screen time use over 1 week. Every time you use a screen for non-work or non-educational purposes, write down when you viewed the screen and for how long.

- o *Remove:* This requires that you remove a source of screen time. For example, delete a social media app or disable your notifications. Alternatively, try a one-day phone detox and see if you can extend it further.
- o *Reduce:* Batch screen time by predetermining a block of time where you will intentionally enjoy a screen. Also, practise deciding what you are going to watch before you start.
- o *Replace:* Removing or reducing screen time will immediately free up your time, energy, and attention. Funnel these resources into the fundamentals of Doing Happy.

2. **Design a MAM. For example,**
   - o Every time I mindlessly unlock my phone, I will write down the time to help me build awareness of my screen time habits. (Note that awareness alone can change behaviour.)
   - o Every time I mindless unlock my phone, I will do 5 push-ups (Fundamental — Exercise).
   - o At 5pm, I will batch my screen time for 30 minutes. Before I start, I will ask myself "What do I want to watch?"
   - o Remove and replace screen time by going to bed 10 minutes earlier every day.

3. **Perform a 3650 forecast:**
   - o 3650 X [Document each time I mindlessly unlock my phone] = The level of *awareness* this builds will *significantly decrease* screen time usage (in the short-term and after 10 years).
   - o 3650 X [5 push-ups every time I mindlessly unlock my phone] = It depends on how many times you mindlessly unlock your

phone. My guess is that after 10 years, you will either do thousands of push-ups or limit your screen time. Both are great.

o 3650 X [Ask "What do I want to watch?" before starting] = The level of *intentionality* this builds will *significantly increase* your enjoyment of screen time (in the short term and after 10 years).

o 3650 X [Replacing 10 minutes of screen time every night with sleep] = 36,500 minutes (608.3 hours/25.3 days) of extra sleep you gain over 10 years.

Chapter 13

The *Do Happy Snapshot*

"If you can't measure it, you can't improve it"
~ Lord Kelvin

Congratulations! We have now covered each of the nine fundamentals. However, the reality is that happiness is not a "set and forget" game. Just like a ship needs to adjust its sails and course to account for changing winds and currents, Doing Happy requires us to regularly review our fundamentals so that we stay on track.

Introducing, the *Do Happy Snapshot*.

It is designed to quickly audit your fundamentals so you can gauge which areas you performing well in and which areas need more attention. It will take you less than a minute and as long as you have something to write on, you can do it anywhere.

The *Do Happy Snapshot*

1. Draw a circle.
2. Divide it into 8 slices.
3. Add a box under it.
4. Label each of the slices with *Exercise, Sleep, Nutrition, Relationships, Nature, Kindness, Gratitude, and Meditation.*
5. Label the box with *Screen time.*
6. Rate yourself out of 10 for each of the fundamentals.
7. For the first 8 fundamentals, the higher the score, the better. However, for screen time, a higher score is worse. If you reduce your screen time score, you can funnel it into one of the other fundamentals.

In less than a minute, you will have a visual representation of how you are performing with each of the fundamentals.

Here is what a *Do Happy Snapshot* could look like:

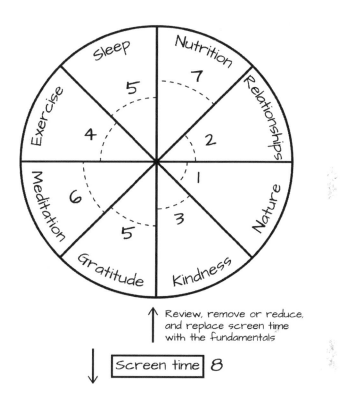

Figure 12

The screen time score is high, while nature and relationships scores are low. In the interest of Doing Happy, I may replace my screen time by calling a friend (relationships) and organising a hike with them (nature).

Dr G's prescription

The power of performing the *Do Happy Snapshot* is that in less than a minute, you gain *awareness*. Once you know where you stand, you can take the necessary action — whether that means staying on course or making a few adjustments.

Turn to the corresponding page of your *Do Happy Workbook*, to complete the following exercise.

1. **Perform a *Do Happy Snapshot*.**

2. **Design a MAM. For example,**
   - When I am feeling low (e.g. sad, depressed, anxious, or worried), I will do a *Do Happy Snapshot*.
   - When I am feeling great (e.g. happy, excited, grateful, or at peace), I will do a *Do Happy Snapshot*.

3. **Perform a 3650 forecast:**
   - 3650 X [*Do Happy Snapshot* when I am feeling low] = Over 10 years, countless moments of awareness that would help me decide what adjustments to make.
   - 3650 X [*Do Happy Snapshot* when I am feeling great] = Over 10 years, countless moments of awareness that would help me identify what works, allowing me to learn and repeat these successful strategies.

Part 3

Intermediate Skills – Psychological Action

"The happiness of your life depends upon the quality of your thoughts: therefore, guard accordingly, and take care that you entertain no notions unsuitable to virtue and reasonable nature."
~ Marcus Aurelius

Our thoughts guide our physical actions, making them crucial to our happiness. *Psychological action* is what we use to understand, influence, and control the quality of our thoughts. Pursuing mastery of our "inner world" represents a significant step towards happiness.

Happiness is like martial arts. You start as a white belt, and progress through blue, purple, and brown until you reach the prestigious black belt. Learning and implementing the nine fundamental physical actions of *Do Happy* takes one from white to blue belt, a level not to be underestimated. A blue belt can defend themselves well in a fight, much like how mastering the fundamentals can equip you to live a significantly happier life. However, having a black belt means that your capabilities are on a whole new level. These psychological actions will put you on a path towards achieving a black belt in happiness. Welcome to the happiness dojo.

Chapter 14

Feelings as a Compass

"Follow your inner compass.
You will be staggered where it takes you"
~ Unknown

When I was little, I used to love playing with my compass. I ran around in circles trying to "trick" the compass to see if it would ever point in the wrong direction. It was arrogant to believe that I could manipulate the relationship between a compass needle and the Earth's magnetic field. Chinese scientists may have invented the compass as early as the 11th or 12th century and it still remains useful today.

When it comes to your mental health, *what's your compass?*

How do you determine "which way to go" and whether you are going "in the right direction"?

There are three compasses that we can use:
1. Feelings
2. Results
3. Values

For most of us, the compass we use would be our feelings. Our feelings guide our behaviour. Feelings can be either pleasant (e.g. happiness, contentment, peace, excitement) or unpleasant (e.g. sadness, depression, anxiety, overwhelm). If it feels good or we expect it to feel good, we will want to do it more. If it feels bad or we expect it to feel bad, we will want to do it less.

In particular, there is a strong tendency to use unpleasant feelings as a compass to guide decisions and actions. Usually, the resulting decisions and actions can be summed up in one word: *avoidance*. As one of my business coaches Francesco used to say, "people tend to run from pain and walk towards pleasure." Whether unpleasant or pleasant, feelings by their very nature are fleeting.

Doesn't it seem risky to make decisions based on
something that changes from moment to moment?

Years ago, I organised a charity event and was the emcee. I took a deep breath, held the microphone, and delivered my carefully crafted welcome speech to 300 people. I bombed. Short of having tomatoes thrown at me and being booed off stage, it could not have gone worse. Most of the audience ignored me, continuing to chat amongst themselves and the small minority who were listening just smiled sympathetically because there is something intrinsically entertaining, or at least engaging, about watching someone fail in public. This experience confirmed all my fears about public speaking, leaving me deeply embarrassed. I avoided public speaking for years to avoid feeling that way again.

Billionaire investor Warren Buffet once said, "Imagine working on just one skill that could raise your value by 50 percent. That one skill is public speaking." For years, I *avoided* working on this skill because I was afraid. I was using my feelings as a compass. I decided to confront my fears and used public speaking as form of "pressure testing" (I explain this in *Chapter 18: Get out of Your Own Way*). I wanted to catch up on lost time so I spoke, a lot. Despite the discomfort and fear, public speaking has become a powerful tool for personal and professional development. It has introduced me to inspiring people, helped me to develop valuable skills, and opened doors to life-changing opportunities. I even get paid to speak now!

Remember our definition of happiness:

Happiness =
The actions (physical, psychological and perspectival) that contribute to a full, rich and meaningful life.

Public speaking became a form of happiness for me. It was allowing me to have a full, rich, and meaningful life.

Anything in life that is worthwhile, whether it's being a great Mum or Dad, looking after your ageing parents, earning a promotion, reaching a certain income, becoming financially free, building a successful business, or sustaining a happy marriage, will generate a full range of feelings. Sometimes it will feel good. Sometimes it won't. That's normal. Given the fluctuating nature of our feelings, they don't make for a useful compass to guide future behaviour.

However, you can use your feelings as a compass in a wise fashion. All you need to do is apply the right dose of psychological and physical action.

What would I rather feel?

The answer to this question can serve as your compass. Like a compass, it will provide direction (i.e. what to *do*) with no guarantee of the destination (i.e. what you will feel). Just because you go north doesn't mean you will end up at the North Pole. You may end up drowning in the ocean, because you can't control your feelings. Nevertheless, determining what you would rather feel provides direction for your actions. The trick is to treat your desired feeling as a compass to guide you, rather than a destination to get to.

Treat your desired feeling as a compass to guide direction,
rather than a destination to get to.

Let's look at how this works in practice:

Context: You've been invited to a party	
Feel	Social Anxiety
Think	"I don't want to go… there are going to be a lot of people I don't know… I don't want everyone looking at me and thinking that I am a loner… I don't want to talk to anyone."
Do	Stay home and avoid the party.

If we let unpleasant feelings automatically guide what we do, it can dramatically affect the quality of your life. For example, social anxiety might lead you to stay home and miss the chance to meet the love of your life, or simply make a new friend. If we are using our feelings as a compass to drive what we do, we have to carefully consider the consequences as they could be significant.

If you are not satisfied with your "compass", pick another one.

Picking another compass

Next time you are feeling something unpleasant, ask these three questions.

1. ***What would I rather feel?***
    The answer to this question becomes your *new compass*. This is a form of psychological action as even though the question is about your feelings, you are actually changing your thinking. The next question is:

2. ***If I was feeling [Insert answer from above], what would I be thinking?***
    This is also a form psychological action. A question is a great way to trigger higher-quality thinking. Follow up with:

3. ***If I was feeling [Insert answer from above], what would I be doing?***
    This reflects on the physical actions that you could take to feel a certain way. Whatever the answer to this question, go *do* it!

Once you decide how you would rather feel, the more ideas that you can generate for each of the follow-up questions, the more options you have to *Do Happy*.

Let's revisit the previous example with a new compass.

Context: You've been invited to a party	
Feel	Social Anxiety
What would I rather feel? (Change the compass)	Confidence
If I was feeling confident, what would I be thinking?	"I am going to charm the hell out of the people at this party… maybe if there is some music at the party, I can show off the robot dance I have been working on in the shower."
If I was feeling confident, what would I be doing?	I would wear my socks with avocados on it and introduce myself to 5 strangers at the party without having a drop of alcohol.
Do Happy	Now for the fun bit. Get your avocado socks on and go meet some new humans! Don't forget to bust out the robot if the opportunity presents itself.

You may still *feel* anxious, but you can *think* and *do* confidence. Even if you wear the avocado socks, talk to a few people and do the robot, you may still feel anxious. That's ok. You can't control that. You are still committing to actions (psychological and physical) that are leading you to a full, rich, and meaningful life. You are Doing Happy, or rather Doing Confidence. The feelings will sort themselves out. Given feelings, thoughts, and actions are all linked, you will probably end up feeling quite confident anyway. Regardless, treat the feeling of confidence as a compass to guide you rather than a destination to get to.

Another example that shows the power of a new compass.

Context: Criticised by employer for a mistake	
Feel	Anger
What would I rather feel? (Change the compass)	Calm
If I was feeling calm, what would I be thinking?	"Once the emotions settle down, I can sit down and think about whether there is anything to learn from my boss' feedback. Until then, I will give him the benefit of the doubt. Either he is right and I need to change or he is wrong, and he is just having an off day."
If I was feeling calm, what would I be doing?	Speaking slowly, breathing deeply and asking questions to better understand the situation before jumping to conclusions.
Do Happy	Now it's time to commit to action. The initial feeling of anger could have guided you, but it may have led to a disastrous situation, like saying something to your boss that you later regret. Doing Calm seems like a better option.

I had a patient who was once criticised by their employer. She was Furious, with a capital F. She took the day off and the next day, her plan was to resign. Her unpleasant feelings were guiding her to a big and potentially irreversible decision.

She didn't like being angry. She admitted to saying and doing some regretful things in the past when she was angry. We took the time to explore what she would rather feel. Her answer? Composed. We explored what a composed person would think and do in this situation.

After she settled down, she decided to stay. She needed the money and most of the time, she actually enjoyed her work and the people she worked with. Composure was a better compass than anger.

Be careful of using unpleasant feelings as a compass. *The more intense the feelings are, the more careful we need to be.* Take ownership and practise regularly choosing your own compass by asking: "What would I rather feel?"

Dr G's prescription

Feelings, like the weather, are unpredictable and unreliable as a guide if left on autopilot. However, by learning to *choose* our desired feelings, we can use them as a compass to guide our actions and lead a happier life.

Turn to the corresponding page of your *Do Happy Workbook*, to complete the following exercise.

1. **Next time you are feeling something unpleasant, answer the following questions:**
    o What is happening (i.e. the context)?
    o What are you feeling?
    o What would you rather feel? (Psychological action)
    o If you were feeling [insert answer above], what would you be thinking? (Psychological action)
    o If you were feeling [insert answer above], what would you be doing? (Physical action)
    o Time to *Do Happy*. Go *do* it.

2. **Design a MAM. For example,**
    o Ask yourself, "What would I rather feel?" each time you feel something unpleasant.

3. **Perform a 3650 forecast:**
    o 3650 X [Asking "What would I rather feel?" each time you feel something unpleasant] = Consistently choosing a better compass that will guide better decisions and actions over the next 10 years. The destination? A much happier place.

Chapter 15

Results as a Compass

"Happiness is highest on the hierarchy of goals, the end toward which all other ends lead. Wealth, fame, admiration, and all other goals are subordinate and secondary to happiness; whether our desires are material or social, they are means toward one end: happiness."

~ Dr Tal Ben-Shamar

Why do you do anything?
- Why do you put your clothes on in the morning?
- Why do you aim for that promotion?
- Why do you smoke? If you don't smoke, why not?
- Why did you start that business?
- Why did you buy that house? Or that stock?
- Why do you spend time with your family?
- Why do you hire a coach or a mentor?
- Why did you eat the last brownie? No, I am not watching you.

Everything we do is in the expectation of a certain result. Life is the pursuit of results. If life is the pursuit of results, happiness is *the* result. Everything we do is in the hope that it leads us to a better life and ultimately, happiness.

If life is the pursuit of results, happiness is <u>the</u> result.

Happiness represents the actions, physical, psychological and perspectival, that contribute to a full, rich, and meaningful life. If the ultimate result *is* happiness, this can take many forms.

- *Personal results*: being a great parent, becoming fit, caring for ageing parents, or giving to charity.
- *Professional results*: reaching a certain income, gaining a promotion, or building a reputation within your industry.
- *External results*: cars, houses, wealth, or status.
- *Internal results*: cultivating gratitude and inner peace or letting go of shame and guilt.
- *Emotional results*: feeling happy, satisfied and fulfilled with life.

If life is the pursuit of results, with the ultimate result being happiness itself, why not make results the compass?

Feel-Think-Do-*Results* (FTDR) Model

In the *Theory* section, I introduced the Feel-Think-Do (FTD) model. Up until now, we have been primarily using feelings as a compass for what we think (psychological action) and do (physical action). For example, the fundamentals are designed to significantly increase your chances of feeling better. Now it's time to introduce another layer to this model, *results* (See Figure 13). This is the Feel-Think-Do-Results (FTDR) model.

Note that this is not part of the traditional Cognitive Behavioural Therapy (CBT) model as it is something I have developed over the years to help my patients and clients.

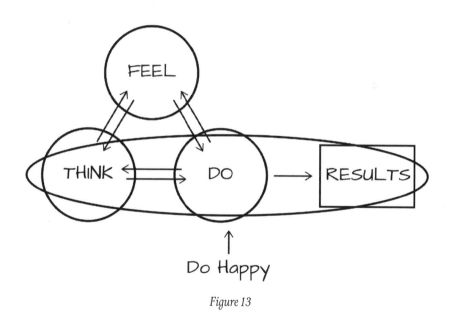

Figure 13

A common misconception is that happiness requires you to *feel* good all the time. This is a recipe for failure and ironically, unhappiness.

"A life spent in pursuit of those [happy] feelings is, in the main, unsatisfying. In fact, the harder we pursue pleasurable feelings, the more we are likely to suffer from anxiety and depression."
~ Russ Harris

The FTDR acknowledges feelings as a useful compass, but prioritises *results*. Doing Happy now focusses on the actions that guide you towards the results you want in life. Exciting, right? Happiness is about the actions that will drive you towards a full, rich, and meaningful life — a result that is achievable and worth fighting for.

Results, unlike momentary feelings, are much more stable and change only if you choose to change them. Therefore, they serve as a useful compass. As you move towards your desired result, you may experience a range of feelings, from pleasant to unpleasant and everything in between. Regardless of these fluctuations, like a ship's destination that remains constant despite a storm, the desired result remains unchanged.

Reading non-fiction books has transformed my life. It is a beautiful thing to be able to download decades worth of wisdom from the author in return for spending 10 to 20 hours reading. I wanted to pay it forward and have this impact on someone else. When I decided to write my first book, the one you are reading now, it is a result that directly aligned with my vision for living a full, rich, and meaningful life.

Do you think I felt happy the whole time I was writing it? If you want the raw truth, ask my wife. At times I felt happy, but often I was frustrated with the process, doubting whether it was worth writing. Occasionally, I felt proud when I wrote something I considered insightful. It has been a beautiful metaphor for the full sensory and emotional experience that is life. I know one thing for sure — it was worth it.

What do I want?

In the previous chapter we explored using feelings as a compass by asking, "What would I rather feel?" Now we ask a different question, *"What do I want?"*

Asking this question is a form of psychological action because it shifts your thinking and clarifies the result you are aiming for. Once you decide what you want, you can reverse engineer the actions needed to achieve it. Then of course, you can *Do Happy* by actually committing to those actions.

Results can take three forms:
1. Processes
2. Milestones
3. In-the-moment

Processes

Process results represent actions that are committed to on a regular basis.

Examples of process results:
- Running for 30 minutes a day
- Doing 10 push-ups a day
- Meditating for 15 minutes a day
- Reviewing your investments once a month
- Gratitude journaling about 5 things every day
- Having a date night with your partner once a week

Milestones

Milestone results have clear destinations, so you know exactly when you have arrived.

Examples of milestone results:
- Running a 42km marathon
- Writing a 50,000-word book
- Buying a house
- Getting 10 clients

All milestone results require a carefully designed process to get you there.

- Running a 42km marathon (milestone) requires a 20-week running program (process).
- Writing a 65,000 word book called *Do Happy* (milestone) required writing 700 words a day to produce a draft (process) and then 1-2 hours a day of editing until completion (process).
- Buying a house (milestone) may require researching suitable properties every day (process) and attending open inspections every weekend (process).
- Getting 10 clients (milestone) may require working on your product every day (process), posting on social media once a day (process) and reaching out to 5 people every day to tell them about your product (process).

In-the-moment

In-the-moment results represent what you want out of a certain situation *as it happens*. For example, in the middle of an argument with your partner, you might decide that the result you want is a civilised conversation that avoids blame and seeks a solution.

In the moment results can also be a feeling. When we use feelings as a compass, the feelings become the in-the-moment results that guide our behaviour. In this context, asking the question "What would you rather feel?" is the same as asking, "What do you want?" Therefore, a *feeling can be the result*.

Using results as a compass

Regardless of whether it's a process, a milestone, or an in-the-moment result, it all starts with the question, "What do I want?" Once you answer this question, you can determine the actions required to achieve it and proceed to *Do Happy*.

Three steps to use results as a compass:

1. **What do I want?**
   This will determine your desired result which could either be a process, a milestone, or an in-the-moment result.

2. **What can I think (psychological action) and do (physical action) that will drive me towards what I want?**
   - If it's a process result, the process *is* what you will do.
   - If it's a milestone result, this question will determine the processes that are required for you to move towards your goal.
   - If it's an in-the-moment result, this question will determine the psychological and physical actions that you can commit to in real time.

3. ***Do Happy***
   Whatever the answer is to the previous question, go *do* it and start building a life that is full, rich, and meaningful.

Similar to our feelings, treat results like a compass and not a destination. A compass provides direction for your behaviour, while a destination suggests a fixed endpoint, which isn't always guaranteed. You cannot control the result, only your actions. Given that *Do Happy* is about taking full ownership of your mental health, focus on the 3 P's of action that you can control — physical, psychological, and perspectival.

Treat results like a compass to guide direction, not destination.

Dr G's prescription

Life is the pursuit of results. Happiness is *the* result. Make the results the compass by asking, "What do I want?"

Turn to the corresponding page of your *Do Happy Workbook*, to complete the following exercise.

1. **What do I want? Think of a process, milestone, and in-the-moment result.**
   o Process result: _____
   o Milestone result: _____
   o In-the-moment result: _____

2. **What can I *think* (psychological action) and *do* (physical action) that will drive me towards what I want?** Answer this question for each of the results you want to work towards.

3. ***Do Happy:*** Whatever the answer, go *do* it and actively start building a life that is full, rich, and meaningful.

4. **Design a MAM. For example,**
   ○ Ask yourself, "What do I want?" at the start of each day.

5. **Perform a 3650 forecast:**
   ○ 3650 X [Asking "What do I want?" at the start of each day] = Consistently choosing results as a daily compass will guide better decisions and actions over the next 10 years.

Chapter 16

Values as a Compass

"Your beliefs become your thoughts, your thoughts become your words, your words become your actions, your actions become your habits, your habits become your values, your values become your destiny."
~ Mahatma Gandhi

The world is full of people who pursue and achieve worthy results. Unfortunately, some of these people are miserable.

» The doctor or nurse that saves lives at work and yet hates their life.
» The teacher who inspires the next generation to dream at work but still lacks fulfillment.
» The millionaire with the successful business that lacks meaning and purpose.

In the previous chapter, we explored the concept of using results as a compass. It's crucial to understand that results are much more useful as a guide rather than a final destination. Reflect on a time when you set a goal and achieved it — what happened next? If you are like most, you *immediately* set another goal. This pattern illustrates that, from a happiness perspective, the result itself is less important than the rich, full and meaningful journey it offers.

Thankfully, there is a way to have your cake and eat it too. *Values.*

What are values?

Values are "one's judgement of what is important in your life". Research suggests that what we value is a "combination of genetic heritage and the impact of exposure to multiple social environments, such as family, the education system, community and society at large". In other words, our genetics and how they interact with the environment determine what we consider to be important.

Genetics + Environment → Values

Values are stable. They don't come and go like feelings. They can change, but only slowly, usually over years. For example, in my teens and twenties, I valued achievement and service. I was singularly focussed on becoming a doctor and doing charity work. Now in my thirties, I value happiness, service, growth, family, and entrepreneurship. Although my genetics haven't changed, my environment has and I have been exposed to various experiences. My values have slowly shifted to match the person I am slowly becoming. Despite these changes, the inherent stability of values provides an exciting opportunity to use values as a compass to guide our actions.

To understand the essence of values, we can learn from the biggest companies in the world. All organisations have a set of values. For example, Microsoft values respect, integrity and accountability. They say "our values... serve as a declaration of *how* we treat each other, our customers, and our partners." These values guide *how* they behave within the company.

Check out Apple's set of core values:
- We believe that we're on the face of the Earth to make great products.
- We believe in the simple, not the complex.
- We believe that we need to own and control the primary technologies behind the products we make.
- We participate only in markets where we can make a significant contribution.
- We believe in saying no to thousands of projects so that we can really focus on the few that are truly important and meaningful to us.
- We believe in deep collaboration and cross-pollination of our groups, which allow us to innovate in a way that others cannot.
- We don't settle for anything less than excellence in every group in the company, and we have the self-honesty to admit when we're wrong and the courage to change.

You can see how the above values guide Apple products. The quality (see value 1) and simplicity of their products (see value 2) has been prominent from its inception. I still remember when they introduced the iPod with the tagline, "1,000 songs in your pocket". It was a stroke of genius.

Do you think the team at Apple will arrive at work next Monday and say, "I don't *feel* like creating a great product today"? Even if they feel that way, their values will guide their behaviour and ensure that they keep creating world class products.

Amazon's values are:
- Customer obsession rather than competitor focus.
- Passion for invention.
- Commitment to operational excellence.
- Long-term thinking.

Once I ordered a business book via Amazon at 10:30pm on a Tuesday night. The book was at my front door by 12:30pm the next day. If that doesn't show "customer obsession", I don't know what does. This level of services is a testament to how deeply these values guide their behaviour.

If an organisation can have a set of values that drives them towards incredible results, why can't we as individuals lean on our own values in the same way?

The premise of *Do Happy* is that it's possible to be happy *all the time*. Values are powerful because, no matter what is happening or how we are feeling, we can *always* align our actions with them. Given values represent what's important in our life, living into them through our actions will undoubtedly contribute to a full, rich and meaningful life.

Feel-Think-Do-*Values*-Results (FTDVR) model

Reflecting on our values is a form of psychological action, while acting on them is a form of physical action. Values are so important that they deserve their own place on the *Do Happy* framework.

Let's review the evolution of Doing Happy so far.

We first explored the Feel-Think-Do (FTD) model as providing the foundation for *Doing Happy* (Figure 14).

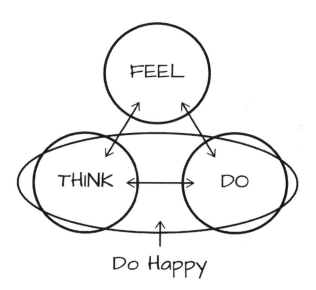

Figure 14

Then we explored the utility of using results as a compass to drive behaviour (Figure 15).

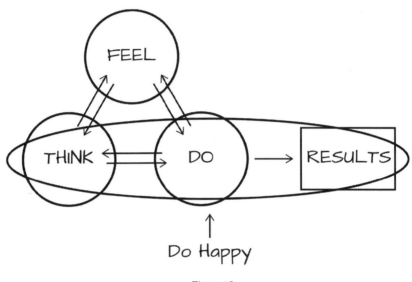

Figure 15

The FTDR model is exciting but it is still flawed. While we can define what we want and reverse engineer the actions required to get there, many people who follow this approach remain unhappy. The world is full of miserable people who have achieved their goals. Why? *Because they are in conflict with their values.*

> *For those that achieve big results in their lives and remain unhappy, there is likely a conflict in values.*

For example, if you value family and connection, becoming a successful CEO of a multinational company, a desired result, at the expense of your family will almost guarantee unhappiness.

Let's include values in the *Do Happy* framework (Figure 16).

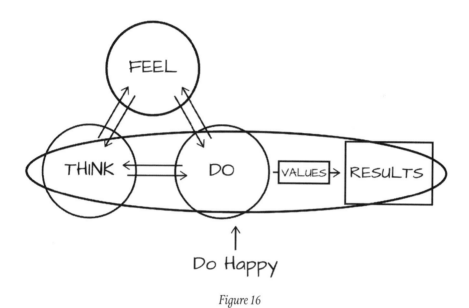

Figure 16

Isn't it beautiful?

The result provides the destination. The purpose of the destination is not as an endpoint itself but rather, the meaningful experience it provides us on the way. There are many ways to reach a destination. Our values will allow us to choose the route that aligns with what is important to us. By doing so, we can live according to our values *all the time* whilst pursuing our desired results. Voila! Have your cake and eat it too.

Jenny was referred to me after suffering for decades with anxiety. She knew she was destined for a better life but she was stuck in a vicious cycle of *reacting* to her unpleasant feelings. If something felt unpleasant, she avoided it. Over the years, most things started to make her feel anxious. Imagine the type of results you get in your life when you avoid pretty much everything actually in your life.

She had never considered taking a results and values based approach. We started with her values. When we audited her life, we found that she was the best version of herself when she was overcoming adversity. "Overcome" became one of her core values. The irony was that the anxiety that she had suffered for all these years was the very thing that she needed to lean into her value of overcoming. Overcoming requires discomfort. Otherwise, what is there to overcome?

Overcoming discomfort is not easy. We needed a way to predictably induce her anxiety so that we could practise her value of overcoming. The answer? Public speaking. For weeks, our sessions involved her speaking on various topics. The topic was irrelevant. The discomfort of speaking is what mattered. The first time she spoke her face went red, she was restless, and she could barely string a sentence together. By the seventh time, she was smiling like someone without a mortgage. When I asked her why she was smiling, she replied, "I am actually starting to enjoy this." This is the power of leaning into our values and not reacting to our feelings.

A few months later she spoke in front of a large family gathering to celebrate her father's birthday. She was feeling, in her words, "terrified." She took a deep breath and decided to overcome. By the end of the speech, she was met with applause and hugs. A few years prior, she was offered a chance to speak at her Mum's funeral. She declined the offer. She felt too anxious. Her unpleasant feelings had stopped her from living a full, rich and meaningful life. The speech she gave at her father's birthday was her redemption speech.

After months of practising her value of overcoming, something interesting happened. The relationship she had with her feeling of anxiety changed. She didn't see it as a bad thing anymore. She was starting to like it. Every time she was anxious, it gave her an opportunity to overcome. These days she is pursuing a different result. She wants to be a professional speaker. She wants to share her story to help others avoid the suffering she experienced, and she aims to get paid for it.

This is the same person who was terrified of public speaking and didn't want to leave the house. A results and values based approach changed her life. If you ask her, she would tell you she's *happy*.

Values can often conflict with feelings. For example, you may value kindness but feel hurt and angry with someone. Despite these feelings, you can still act kindly. What feels good may not always be in your best interest. When people act according to their values, they often experience a sense of alignment, even if they feel something unpleasant in the moment.

Discovering your values

It's time to determine what you value. I often have the privilege of guiding my patients and clients through this journey. If it helps, picture the two of us doing this together over tea. I will be drinking a dirty chai. What are you drinking?

Set aside 15-30 minutes.

Step 1: Print

Go to the corresponding page of your *Do Happy Workbook*. There you will find a list of values. (Source: www.saturdaygift.com)

Step 2: Current values

Using a coloured highlighter, mark the values that are important to you *now*. Similar to an organisation and its values, these are the values that guide your behaviour already. You may not always live according to them but that's okay, you still consider them important. Keep in mind that all values are good. There are no "bad" values right? Avoid the temptation to highlight everything. If it helps, skim through the list first to get a sense of it, then go over it again to highlight the values that are truly important to you.

Here are mine highlighted:

Abundance	**Contribution**	Freedom	Meaning	Simplicity
Acceptance	Control	Friendship	Moderation	Sincerity
Accomplishment	Cooperation	Fun	Motivation	Skillfulness
Accountability	Courage	**Generosity**	Obedience	Solitude
Accuracy	Courtesy	Giving	Openness	Speed
Achievement	**Creativity**	Goodness	Optimism	**Spirituality**
Adaptability	Credibility	Grace	Order	Stability
Adventure	Curiosity	**Gratitude**	Organization	Status
Affection	Decisiveness	Growth	Originality	Stewardship
Alertness	Dedication	**Happiness**	Passion	Strength
Ambition	Dependability	Hard Work	**Patience**	Structure
Assertiveness	Determination	Harmony	Patriotism	Success
Attentive	Devotion	Health	**Peace**	Support
Authenticity	Dignity	**Honesty**	Playfulness	Surprise
Awareness	**Discipline**	Honor	Poise	Sustainability
Balance	Diversity	**Humility**	Positivity	Teamwork
Beauty	Efficiency	**Humor**	Power	Temperance
Boldness	Empathy	Imagination	Productivity	Thankful
Bravery	Endurance	Independence	Professionalism	Thorough
Brilliance	**Energy**	Individuality	Prosperity	**Thoughtful**
Calmness	Enjoyment	Inner Harmony	Purpose	Timeliness
Capable	Enthusiasm	Innovation	Quality	Tolerance
Careful	Equality	Insightful	Recognition	Toughness
Caring	Ethical	Inspiring	Respect	Traditional
Certainty	**Excellence**	Integrity	Responsibility	Tranquility
Challenge	Excitement	Intelligence	Restraint	Transparency
Charity	**Experience**	Intuitive	Results-oriented	Trustworthy
Cleanliness	Expertise	Joy	Rigor	Understanding
Clear	Exploration	Justice	Security	Uniqueness
Clever	Fairness	**Kindness**	Self-actualization	Unity
Comfort	Faith	Knowledge	Self-development	Vision
Commitment	Fame	Lawful	Self-reliance	Vitality
Communication	Family	Leadership	Self-respect	Wealth
Community	Fearless	**Learning**	Selfless	Welcoming
Compassion	Fidelity	Logic	Sensitivity	Winning
Competence	Fitness	Love	Serenity	Wisdom
Confidence	Focus	Loyalty	**Service**	
Consistency	Foresight	Mastery	Sharing	
Contentment	Forgiveness	Maturity	Silence	

Source: www.saturdaygift.com

Step 3: Aspirational values

With a different colour, highlight the values that you want to aspire towards. These are values that you consider important but don't really embody yet.

Here are mine highlighted in a darker shade:

Abundance	**Contribution**	Freedom	Meaning	Simplicity
Acceptance	Control	Friendship	Moderation	Sincerity
Accomplishment	Cooperation	Fun	Motivation	Skillfulness
Accountability	Courage	**Generosity**	Obedience	Solitude
Accuracy	Courtesy	Giving	Openness	Speed
Achievement	**Creativity**	Goodness	Optimism	**Spirituality**
Adaptability	Credibility	Grace	Order	Stability
Adventure	Curiosity	**Gratitude**	Organization	Status
Affection	Decisiveness	Growth	Originality	Stewardship
Alertness	Dedication	**Happiness**	Passion	Strength
Ambition	Dependability	Hard Work	**Patience**	Structure
Assertiveness	Determination	Harmony	Patriotism	Success
Attentive	Devotion	Health	**Peace**	Support
Authenticity	Dignity	**Honesty**	Playfulness	Surprise
Awareness	**Discipline**	Honor	Poise	Sustainability
Balance	Diversity	**Humility**	Positivity	Teamwork
Beauty	Efficiency	**Humor**	Power	Temperance
Boldness	Empathy	Imagination	Productivity	Thankful
Bravery	Endurance	Independence	Professionalism	Thorough
Brilliance	**Energy**	Individuality	Prosperity	**Thoughtful**
Calmness	Enjoyment	Inner Harmony	Purpose	Timeliness
Capable	Enthusiasm	Innovation	Quality	Tolerance
Careful	Equality	Insightful	Recognition	Toughness
Caring	Ethical	Inspiring	Respect	Traditional
Certainty	**Excellence**	Integrity	Responsibility	Tranquility
Challenge	Excitement	Intelligence	Restraint	Transparency
Charity	**Experience**	Intuitive	Results-oriented	Trustworthy
Cleanliness	Expertise	Joy	Rigor	Understanding
Clear	Exploration	Justice	Security	Uniqueness
Clever	Fairness	**Kindness**	Self-actualization	Unity
Comfort	Faith	Knowledge	Self-development	Vision
Commitment	Fame	Lawful	Self-reliance	Vitality
Communication	Family	Leadership	Self-respect	Wealth
Community	Fearless	**Learning**	Selfless	Welcoming
Compassion	Fidelity	Logic	Sensitivity	Winning
Competence	Fitness	Love	Serenity	Wisdom
Confidence	Focus	Loyalty	**Service**	
Consistency	Foresight	Mastery	Sharing	
Contentment	Forgiveness	Maturity	Silence	

Step 4: 7 people you admire.

Write down seven people that you admire and *why*. With these reflections in mind, use a different colour to highlight any values that these people embody. You may notice an overlap between your current or aspirational values with these ones. That's great! This shows consistency in what you value and consider to be important.

Here are mine in the darkest highlight:

Abundance	**Contribution**	Freedom	Meaning	Simplicity
Acceptance	Control	Friendship	Moderation	Sincerity
Accomplishment	Cooperation	Fun	Motivation	Skillfulness
Accountability	Courage	**Generosity**	Obedience	Solitude
Accuracy	Courtesy	Giving	Openness	Speed
Achievement	**Creativity**	Goodness	Optimism	**Spirituality**
Adaptability	Credibility	Grace	Order	Stability
Adventure	Curiosity	**Gratitude**	Organization	Status
Affection	Decisiveness	Growth	Originality	Stewardship
Alertness	Dedication	**Happiness**	Passion	Strength
Ambition	Dependability	Hard Work	**Patience**	Structure
Assertiveness	Determination	Harmony	Patriotism	Success
Attentive	Devotion	Health	**Peace**	Support
Authenticity	Dignity	**Honesty**	Playfulness	Surprise
Awareness	**Discipline**	Honor	Poise	Sustainability
Balance	Diversity	**Humility**	Positivity	Teamwork
Beauty	Efficiency	**Humor**	Power	Temperance
Boldness	Empathy	Imagination	Productivity	Thankful
Bravery	Endurance	Independence	Professionalism	Thorough
Brilliance	**Energy**	Individuality	Prosperity	**Thoughtful**
Calmness	Enjoyment	Inner Harmony	Purpose	Timeliness
Capable	Enthusiasm	Innovation	Quality	Tolerance
Careful	Equality	Insightful	Recognition	Toughness
Caring	Ethical	Inspiring	Respect	Traditional
Certainty	**Excellence**	Integrity	Responsibility	Tranquility
Challenge	Excitement	Intelligence	Restraint	Transparency
Charity	**Experience**	Intuitive	Results-oriented	Trustworthy
Cleanliness	Expertise	Joy	Rigor	Understanding
Clear	Exploration	Justice	Security	Uniqueness
Clever	Fairness	**Kindness**	Self-actualization	Unity
Comfort	Faith	Knowledge	Self-development	Vision
Commitment	Fame	Lawful	Self-reliance	Vitality
Communication	Family	Leadership	Self-respect	Wealth
Community	Fearless	**Learning**	Selfless	Welcoming
Compassion	Fidelity	Logic	Sensitivity	Winning
Competence	Fitness	Love	Serenity	Wisdom
Confidence	Focus	Loyalty	**Service**	
Consistency	Foresight	Mastery	Sharing	
Contentment	Forgiveness	Maturity	Silence	

Step 5: Categorise

Now it's time to categorise your values. Draw a table with five columns. Go through your list of highlighted values. Put the first value in the first column. Now move on to the next value. Do you think that this value belongs in the same group as the first value? If so, put it in the first column. If not, start another list in the second column. Keep going until all the values are categorised. For example, if your first value on the list is "balance", put that in the first column. If your second value is "calmness", you may put it under "balance" as they are linked. If, however, your second value is "charity", you will put that in the second column as it is unrelated to "balance". Aim for a maximum of five categories. You can technically have more but it's generally not useful to have more than five. This limit is arbitrary; you can adjust the number of categories based on what works best for you.

Here are mine. You may notice that I have added a few things to tailor these values to myself.

Column 1	Column 2	Column 3	Column 4	Column 5
Freedom "from"	Charity	Insightful	Family	Accountability
Acceptance	Community	Learning	Connection	Commitment
Adaptability	Contribution	Pursuing mastery	Community	Consistency
Awareness	Generosity	Thoughtful	Affection	Discipline
Balance	Kindness	Uniqueness (push the envelope)	Caring	Excellence
Calmness	Service (without attachment)		Communication	Focus
Clear		Honesty	Compassion	Simplicity
Contentment	Teach	Humility	Trustworthy	Challenge
Energy	Peace in motion	Thoughtful	Fun and playfulness	Clever
Gratitude		Transparency	Unconditional love	Creativity
Happiness		Experience		Experience
Humour				Craftmanship
Patience				Teach
Peace				Leverage
Simplicity				Wealth
Spirituality				
Wisdom				

Step 6: Unify

For each of the categories, choose a word that best represents the common theme and unifies the whole category. You may find that one of the values within the category will summarise the whole category. For example, "Happiness" is in my first column *and* unifies the whole category as well. Here are mine.

Happiness	Service	Growth	Family	Entrepreneurship
Freedom "from"	Charity	Insightful	Family	Accountability
Acceptance	Community	Learning	Connection	Commitment
Adaptability	Contribution	Pursuing mastery	Community	Consistency
Awareness	Generosity	Thoughtful	Affection	Discipline
Balance	Kindness	Uniqueness (push the envelope)	Caring	Excellence
Calmness	Service (without attachment)	Honesty	Communication	Focus
Clear	Teach	Humility	Compassion	Simplicity
Contentment	Peace in motion	Thoughtful	Trustworthy	Challenge
Energy		Transparency	Fun and playfulness	Clever
Gratitude		Experience	Unconditional love	Creativity
Happiness				Experience
Humour				Craftmanship
Patience				Teach
Peace				Leverage
Simplicity				Wealth
Spirituality				
Wisdom				

Step 7: Add meaning

For each of these values, write a supporting statement to explain why it's important to you.

Happiness	Prioritise happiness for myself and everyone around me, in that order.
Service	I am blessed with the opportunities and skills to make a difference in the world. I am obligated to act on this with a smile on my face.
Growth	I will invest in myself as I will grow faster than any other asset. As I grow, I will try to bring as many people as possible with me.
Family	I am nothing without the incredible people in my life. I will always give them my most valuable resource, my time.
Entrepreneurship	Create work that I am proud of, that helps other people.

Congratulations! If you have got this far and done the work, you should have a list of values that resonate with you. Don't worry about getting it perfect; consider this your first draft. You can review and refine it periodically. What's important is to *start the practice of living according to your values.*

Using values as a compass

Regardless of the results you work towards, lean into your values and you will experience a beautiful sense of *alignment* with what you do, who you are, and what's important to you.

Three steps to using values as a compass:

1. **What do I want?**
   This will determine your desired result which could either be a process, a milestone or an in-the-moment result.

2. **What can I think (psychological action) and do (physical action) that will drive me towards what I want?**
   This will determine the actions that will drive you towards what you want.

3. **What do my values say I should do?**
   Repeatedly ask this question to ensure that the above actions *align* with your values.

Dr G's prescription

Values represent what is important in your life. They serve as a powerful compass in your life, particularly when combined with a result worth pursuing.

Turn to the corresponding page of your *Do Happy Workbook*, to complete the following exercise.

1. **If you haven't already, perform the values exercise.**

2. **Design a MAM. For example,**
   o Ask, "What do my values say I should do?", every time you feel something unpleasant.

3. **Perform a 3650 forecast:**
   o 3650 X [Asking, "What do my values say I should do?", every time you feel something unpleasant] = A sense of alignment with what you are doing and what's important to you which will grow deeper and deeper over the next 10 years.

Chapter 17

Flicking the Channel

"All things are created twice. There's a mental or first creation, and a physical or second creation to all things."
~ Dr Stephen Covey

High school camp taught me a lot more than I expected.

In high school, every year we all got on a bus and went to the same place in Cowes on Phillip Island for the much-awaited school camp. We climbed ropes, used compasses to navigate the bush, flirted, and stayed up well past our curfew. One of my funniest memories is waking up and wandering over to the nearby stream to freshen up for the morning. I saw most of my friends knee deep in the water, grabbing handfuls of water to splash on their faces and using the same water to moisten the toothpaste on their brushes before cleaning their teeth. About 10 metres upstream, I saw another friend of mine.

He was half-naked, rubbing a bar of soap all over his
body and using the water to rinse the soap off.

Whether it's where you brush your teeth or what you do to become
happier, what happens upstream matters.

What happens upstream matters.

Remember, life is the pursuit of results and the ultimate result is
happiness. The only thing that can directly change the results in our
lives is action. What happens upstream of our actions? *Our thoughts.*

As Dr Stephen Covey said, "All things are created twice. All things.
Vision is the first creation. For a house it's called the blueprint. For a life
it's called a mission. For a day it's called a goal and a plan. For a parent it's
called a belief in the unseen potential of a child. For all, it is the mental
creation which always precedes the physical, or second, creation." If you
are unsatisfied with the quality of your life, it is likely that the problem
exists upstream, in the mind.

Do you struggle with negative or unhelpful thinking?
» "I'll never be good enough."
» "Nothing ever goes my way."
» "I always mess things up."
» "Everyone is against me."
» "I'll never get over this."
» "I don't deserve to be happy."
» "I can never be happy."

» "I'm a failure."
» "I have no value."
» "Nothing I do is working."
» "It's just too hard."

If all things are created twice, first in the mind and then in reality, what type of reality do thoughts like these lead to?

They may stop you from asking out the love of your life. They may prevent you from taking that leap of faith to start the business you've always dreamt of. They could stop you from asking for a raise. They can keep you stuck in a "safe" job that you hate. Although these are all physical creations, they originate from poorly constructed mental creations. Here lies a life-changing opportunity: by reshaping our thoughts, we can transform our reality.

Do you love who you are?

I used to work with someone who wanted to gain control of their mental health. She had seen a few psychologists and made some progress, but things still weren't quite right. We started with the fundamentals and although there were some improvements, something was missing.

"Do you love who you are?" I asked. If I am helping someone become happier, this has become one of my most important questions.

After much deliberation, she answered.

"No."

"Why not?"

"I don't know. I guess I just don't like who I am."

"Why not? You are an amazing person. Why is it that I can see that but you can't?"

"I am not as amazing as you think."

"Explain."

She took a deep breath and answered to both of us, what was missing despite years of therapy.

"About 9 years ago, I was in a really dark place. Everything was falling apart. My dog died. My parents split up. I was having problems with my boyfriend."

After a big sigh, she continued.

"One night, I was invited to a party. I didn't want to go. I just wasn't in the right headspace. My friends forced me to go so I eventually caved. I ended up drinking myself silly. I can't remember anything from the night."

Shaking her head, she continued.

"The next morning, a friend called me in distress, 'Hey, what were you thinking last night?' A few minutes later, another friend calls me, 'What the hell got into you last night?'"

"What happened?" I asked.

"Well, apparently I had gotten blind drunk and started making out with this guy."

> In tears, she continued: "I cheated on my boyfriend.
> I am a horrible person."

In a period of vulnerability amplified by alcohol, she made a mistake. She made this mistake *9 years ago*. This mistake led her to question her character and, ultimately, her worth. She considered herself unlovable. In her mind, she had all the reasons to justify this belief. For years, she suffered from unhelpful thoughts that reinforced the idea that she was unworthy of love. This mental creation had a ripple effect on *everything* in her life. In particular, it affected each subsequent romantic relationship. Believing that she was not good enough, she would eventually self-sabotage her relationships and find trivial reasons to justify ending them.

The NLP communication model

The Neuro-Linguistic Programming (NLP) communication model, developed by John Grinder and Richard Bandler, helps us understand how we interpret life and its circumstances. It was introduced to me by Dr Marli Watt for whom I am eternally grateful. Since learning it, I have applied it in my own life or taught it to others almost every day.

The NLP communication model explains how we take information from the "outside world" and process it in our "inside world". Once you understand how it works, you can use it to improve the quality of your inside world: your mental creations. This can potentially change *everything* downstream, namely your actions and results, thereby changing your life.

What happens upstream in your mind determines
what happens downstream in your life.

The NLP communication model has been simplified and adapted for the purposes of this book. If you wish to explore this topic in more depth, I suggest doing your own research or engaging with a NLP coach.

The NLP communication model consists of:
1. Circumstances
2. Filters
3. Thoughts
4. Feelings
5. Physiology
6. Actions
7. Results

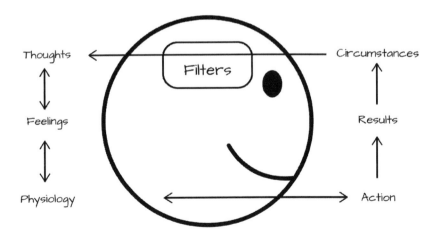

Figure 17

Circumstances

The circumstances represent the facts, data, and events. These are all external. They happen outside the body. These external inputs are received through our five senses — what we see *(visual)*, what we hear *(auditory)*, what we feel *(kinaesthetic)*, what we smell *(olfactory)*, and what we taste *(gustatory)*.

Filters

Our circumstances are received through our five senses and then processed via our filters. Filters are like the gatekeeper for our inside world. Our filters start developing from the moment we are conceived. They include our belief systems (i.e. strong generalisations and assumptions we have about how the world is), our values (i.e. what we consider important), the decisions we have made in the past as well as our past memories. Each of us has a *different* set of filters — they function like a set of prescription glasses. Depending on our "prescription" — and we all have a different one — we "see" and perceive the world differently.

Thoughts

After our circumstances are received via our five senses and processed through our filters, we *make meaning and interpret* the circumstances using our thoughts. Through the lens of our filters, our set of prescription glasses, we make the circumstances mean something. Our filters are why the exact same circumstances can be interpreted differently by different people.

» The father of a child sees their child differently from the mother.

» Comments from an employer are considered constructive criticism by one employee and bullying by another.

» A comment about race is considered racist by one person and humorous by another.

» A crime with six eye witnesses produces six slightly different accounts of what happened.

» A pandemic leads to crippling fear in one person and excitement at the prospect of making a fortune on the stock market for another.

What does this suggest about the nature of the circumstances in our life?

It suggests that the circumstances, the facts, data and events, are *neutral*. It is our thoughts that give it meaning. Taking this perspective allows us to view circumstances as neither good or bad, positive or negative, helpful or unhelpful — they just are.

Circumstances are neutral. Thoughts give it meaning.

Why is this important?

We can create and choose meaning. Through psychological action, we can ensure that the meaning we make is useful and drives us towards the results we want in our life. Everything is created twice, first in our minds and then in reality. Therefore, taking ownership of our ability to create and choose meaning within our minds can be life changing. Later in this chapter, I will show you how.

Let's consider death. Death is a circumstance that will meet us all. Is death neutral?

For many years, I have visited nursing homes to look after who I call my "elderly friends". For most nursing home residents, it is their final stop. Death is a common occurrence in the nursing home. It is fascinating to observe how different people perceive the exact same event, such as the death of an individual, in entirely different ways.

I used to look after a 94-year-old man. Let's call him John. After eight years of worsening dementia, he died.

His wife was grief stricken.

His daughter was relieved that his suffering had come to an end.

His son felt guilty for not visiting often enough.

Many of the extended family members believed "not enough was done" to help him.

The other family members were extremely grateful for the care their relative received.

Some of the nurses who looked after him were sad because they had grown to enjoy the routine of combing his hair in the morning, bathing him, and feeding him.

The staff that had no personal connection to him were indifferent.

Personally, although I never got to meet him before he had dementia, I had heard so many stories about him from his family. He was the oldest of eight children. His Dad died when he was 17 years old which meant that he became the head of the household. He helped his mother raise seven children. When he died, I was proud to have met him. What a legacy!

The exact same *neutral* circumstance, the death of a 94-year-old man in a nursing home, was interpreted differently by everyone, based on their individual filters and what they made it mean.

Feelings

A neutral circumstance is received via our five senses, we process it through our filters and then we make it mean something using our thoughts. Our thoughts directly affect how we feel. It is our thoughts about the circumstance, not the actual circumstance, which determines how we are feeling. As we know from the Feel-Think-Do model, how we feel also affects what we are thinking.

> *It is our thoughts about the circumstance, not the actual circumstance, which determines how we are feeling.*

Physiology

A neutral circumstance is received via our five senses, it is processed through our filters, we make it mean something with our thoughts, which leads us to feel something. This influences our physiology, which refers to our physical bodily functions (e.g. heart rate, breathing rate, pain, muscle tension, appetite and energy levels).

Actions and results

A neutral circumstance occurs, it is processed via our filters, and triggers a chain reaction involving our thoughts, feelings, and physiology. This leads to an action, which can be something you physically do or don't do. The action produces a result. This result becomes a new circumstance which is of course, neutral.

The Two Worlds — Outside and Inside

Once you understand the NLP communication model, you will realise that there is an "outside" world and an "inside" world (see Figure 18). The outside world, which happens externally, relates to the circumstances, actions, and results. The inside world, which happens internally, relates to our filters, thoughts, feelings, and physiology. Pursuing mastery of our inside world is a big step towards taking full ownership of our happiness and ultimately, our life.

"You have power over your mind — not outside events. Realise this, and you will find strength."
~ Marcus Aurelius

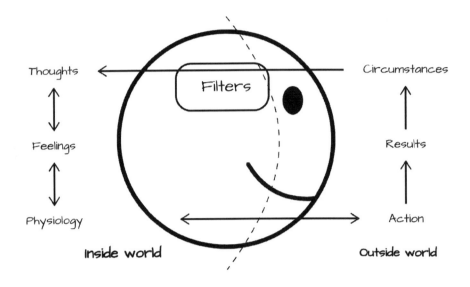

Figure 18

Cultivating a resourceful mind

The NLP communication model is always in play. When faced with a circumstance, the tendency is for people to react, rather than respond. Reactions are instinctive and impulsive, while responses are intentional and deliberate. Which approach do you think would lead to better actions and therefore, better results?

Reacting versus responding

Reactions are actions that are driven by feelings. After something happens, the circumstance, we jump straight to our feelings which drives us to act. As we have discussed in the *Feelings as a compass* chapter, using our automatic feelings as a compass for how we behave is risky. When we react, the circumstance is still filtered and meaning is created with our thoughts. We are simply either unaware or this process happens so quickly that we don't take the time to consider what these thoughts are and whether they are serving us.

Responses are actions that are driven by our conscious thoughts. When we respond, we take the time to pause and intentionally deliberate on what is occurring "upstream". We reflect on what happened, the circumstance, and what we made it mean, our thoughts. This allows us to consider how it made us feel and what action it is driving us to take. We can then evaluate whether this action will lead to the results we want. If the end outcome is going to be unsatisfactory, we can make an adjustment. If reactions are like taking a shortcut through the NLP communication mode, responses are like taking the scenic route. The scenic route allows us the time to be intentional. See Figure 19.

Reactions are actions driven by our feelings.
Responses are actions driven by our conscious thoughts.

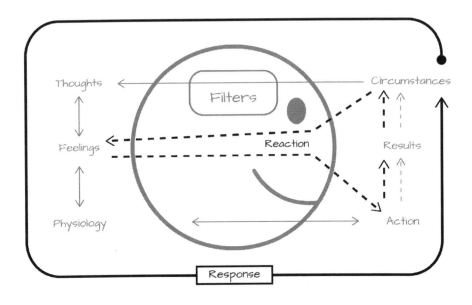

Figure 19

Learning to respond

If what happens upstream of actions and results are our thoughts, then it would be useful to be able to control our thoughts.

Can we control our thoughts?

In the *Theory* section of this book, we explored the nature of our thoughts. Our thoughts can be either unconscious or conscious, the content can be real or imagined, and they can relate to the past, present, and future.

We *can't control our unconscious thoughts,* by definition they lack the ability to be consciously influenced. Russ Harris, in his book *The Happiness Trap*, likens these thoughts to radio channels. For many of us, our unconscious thoughts sound like the "doom and gloom" channel, constantly dwelling on the past, worrying about the future and providing a running commentary of what's wrong with ourselves and the world. These thoughts can be negative and intrusive. Have you ever tried to control or suppress them?

The Distractory Influence Experiment

I was first introduced to this experiment by world-renowned mindfulness expert Professor Craig Hassed. It takes less than a minute to complete.

Close your eyes and bring your attention to something that you can hear consistently in the background. Once you can hear it, try to block it out. Keep trying for about a minute. What happened to the sound?

Most people report that the sound got *louder.* Our unconscious thoughts, particularly the intense and negative ones, are much like this. When we try to control or block them out, they often become louder and more intrusive.

We *can control our conscious thoughts*. This is the essence of psychological action. Imagine you don't like the "music" on your unconsciously trained radio channel. What if you can learn to *"flick the channel"* until you find something that you like listening to? I am loving Sam Smith these days. Let's try to find the channel his music is playing on.

Flicking the channel

My favourite way to flick the channel and utilise our ability to think consciously is to *ask great questions*. If you ask a question, your mind immediately searches for an answer. Do you agree? See what I did there? Oh yes, I did it again. The answers to your questions become your new thoughts.

Flick the channel by asking questions. The answers to your questions, become your new thoughts.

There are four great questions you can ask yourself to help find better "channels" in your mind, thereby allowing you to respond with deliberate actions to the circumstances you face.

1. What happened?
2. What did I make it mean?
3. Is it useful?
4. What else can I make it mean? Ask repeatedly.

What happened?

The answer to this question is the circumstance. Since circumstances represent the *neutral* facts, data, and events, the answer needs to be stripped of all emotion, judgment, and interpretation. A common mistake is to treat the interpretation of a circumstance, as the circumstance itself (see below).

What did I make it mean?

This question is worded intentionally as "*make it mean*" emphasises our ability to *choose* the meaning we attach to a circumstance. *This* is the interpretation that we discussed in the first question. Understanding the subtle difference between this and what actually happened, the circumstance, is key.

Here are some examples to help you make the distinction:

Circumstance (What happened?)	Interpretation (What did I make it mean?)
Today, my boss approached me and discussed a mistake I had made. She spoke in a firm tone.	My boss confronted me about a mistake that I made today. It was totally unfair.
My girlfriend hasn't replied to my text yet. I sent it three hours ago.	My girlfriend hasn't replied to my text. She must think that she has better things to do. If she replies, I am going to make her wait too.
I got 94% for my exam.	I am really smart.
I asked for a promotion and I didn't get it.	I asked for a promotion and I didn't get it. I must not be good enough for the job. I probably don't deserve it anyway.

Is it useful? (i.e. does it drive action towards your desired result?)

The meaning we attach to a neutral circumstance is not necessarily real, true, wise, or useful. Having a thought doesn't make it real. For example, thinking about a pink monkey wearing a batman suit doesn't manifest this magical specimen into reality.

Just because you have a thought, doesn't make it real.

It doesn't matter if a thought is real, true, or even wise. What matters is whether a thought is *useful*. If it is not useful, just flick the channel (see question 4) until you come up with something that is. How do we gauge whether it's useful? Simple. If it is a thought that drives actions that take you towards a result you want, then it's useful. That's a channel worth listening to. If it drives you away, then it's not useful.

Circumstance (What happened?)	Interpretation (What did I make it mean?	Desired Result	Is it useful?
Not considered for a promotion	"I'll never be good enough."	Get a promotion.	No
You asked someone out on a date and they said "No".	"Nothing ever goes my way."	Find long-lasting love.	No
You make a mistake at work.	"I have to figure out a way to be more effective at work."	Grow in my current role	Yes
You make a serious mistake at work.	"I really need to get my act together."	Do a good job at work	Yes
A loved one dies.	"I'll never get over this."	Move past the grief and transform the pain into something purposeful that can help others.	No

What else can I make it mean? Ask repeatedly.

It is time to flick the channel and see what else is playing. Questions naturally provoke your mind to come up with answers. Once you come up with an answer to this question, consider whether you like the sound of this channel. In other words, is it useful or not? With practice, answering this question will help you develop a crucial skill for pursuing mental mastery: the ability to interpret *any* circumstance in a way that is useful and propels you toward the results you want in life.

Repeatedly asking, "What else?" until you have 10, 20, 50, or 100 different answers is a superpower. It helps you cultivate the ability to always find a radio channel that you like listening to, regardless of what has happened. As you generate answers, keep checking whether the meaning you are creating is useful by asking, "Is it useful?" (See Figure 20).

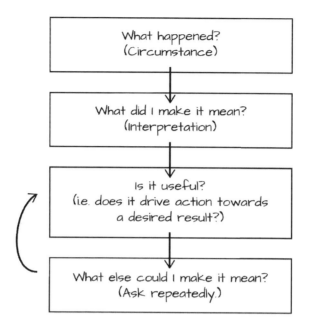

Figure 20

Elias Lebbos is the CEO of Traveller's Aid, a not-for-profit that aims to make society accessible and inclusive to all members of the community. When he and his team moved into their office, instead of having a small whiteboard for brainstorming ideas, he made the *whole wall* a whiteboard. When asked why, he stated that "If the answer is at the corner of the wall and the whiteboard is too small, we may not get there." Repeatedly asking "What else?", will help you "get to the end of the whiteboard" in your mind. It's a skill that will allow you to potentially create *limitless* meaning out of *any* circumstance.

Flicking the channel will allow you to create limitless meaning out of any circumstance.

Here is an example of what getting to the end of the whiteboard in your mind can look like:

What happened?
I am not considered for a promotion.

What did I make it mean?
"I'll never be good enough."

Is it useful? (i.e. does it drive action towards your desired result?)
No. My goal is to get the promotion so thinking that I will "never be good enough" will further sabotage my chances.

What else could I make it mean? Ask repeatedly.

- It's possible that I didn't perform well in the interviews. I will get some formal training to improve my interview skills.
- I am not good enough... yet.
- I need to improve how I market myself at work.
- I am going to use this opportunity to not only become better technically, but improve my sales and marketing skills.
- I think this "No" will lead to a bigger "Yes" later.

- There is a better opportunity for me that is on its way. I need to prepare for it.
- I can ask my boss what they're looking for, address everything they suggest, and then request the promotion again.

There doesn't need to be any limits on this. You are only limited by the resourcefulness of your mind, which is something you can build with practice. Keep checking whether the meaning you are creating is useful by asking: "Is it useful?"

As you practise this skill, you will see an improvement in quantity (i.e. more answers) and quality (i.e. useful answers). It's similar to clicking the "regenerate" button on an AI model like ChatGPT, which allows you to continually refine the answers to your questions until you are satisfied. If the answer is useful, you can give it a thumbs up. This will guide future responses and help you generate similarly useful answers. If the answer isn't useful, you can give it a thumbs down and click the regenerate button to get more options. Eventually, something valuable will emerge. Flicking the channel in your mind requires you to build the skill of doing the same thing, in your mind. This will allow you to *respond* to *any* circumstance.

Dr G's prescription

Everything is created twice. First in your mind, and then in reality. What happens upstream in your mind determines what happens downstream in your life. If you cultivate the skill of flicking the channel and build your capacity to generate limitless meaning from any neutral circumstance, your life will transform. Beware, building the skill of a resourceful mindset will give you superpowers.

Turn to the corresponding page of your *Do Happy Workbook*, to complete the following exercise.

1. **Write down a difficult circumstance in your life. Start with something easy.**

2. **Practise "flicking the channel" by asking these four questions:**
   o What happened?
   o What did I make it mean?
   o Is it useful? (i.e. does it drive action towards your desired result?)
   o What else could I make it mean? Ask repeatedly. Aim for at least 10 answers. If you get to 10, do 10 more. Get to the "end of the whiteboard".

3. **Design a MAM. For example,**
   o Ask, "What happened?" once a day and practise describing the neutral circumstance, stripped of any interpretation.
   o Ask, "What did I make it mean?" and "Is it useful?" once a day to practise responding rather than reacting to circumstances.

4. **Perform a 3650 forecast:**

      o 3650 X [Asking, "What happened?", once a day] = After 10
         years, and likely much sooner, you will gain the wisdom that
         the circumstance is always neutral.

      o 3650 X [Asking, "What did I make it mean?" and "Is it useful?",
         once a day] = 10 years of responding, instead of reacting, which
         will completely change the trajectory of your life.

Chapter 18

Get Out of Your Own Way

*"There are plenty of difficult obstacles in your path.
Don't allow yourself to become one of them."*
~ Ralph Marston

What do you do when you are scared, worried, or anxious about something?

I have posed this question to many individuals, groups, and workplaces over the years. Here are some of the responses.

» "Run away... escape."
» "Ignore it."
» "Try to forget about it."
» "Go to sleep."
» "Talk to my Mum."
» "Exercise."
» "Put some music on."
» "Honestly, I have some wine. Sometimes a lot of wine."

» "I shut myself off from the world. I try to avoid it at all costs."

The underlying theme in all of these answers can be summarised in one word: *Avoid*. When faced with something unpleasant, our natural instinct is to move away from it.

It is a survival mechanism that originates from our evolutionary history. Unpleasant and uncomfortable feelings like fear and anxiety were extremely useful for our ancestors because they signalled danger. During those times, there *was* legitimate danger. If you weren't careful, you could have been chased and killed by a lion. As friend and founder of Let'sTALK Jetha Devapura says, "It would be like living in a zoo, with all the gates open." In the past, fear and anxiety kept people alive. These days, instead of lions, we have emails.

This survival circuitry still exists within us, but often it functions like an outdated software that is due for an update. Humans are designed for survival, not happiness. If you were a caveman in the stone age 20,000 years ago, you did not have the luxury of contemplating what it means to live a full, rich, and meaningful life.

Humans are designed for survival, not happiness.

Is the snake real?

When we experience an unpleasant feeling, we have an aversion to it. Why? We interpret it as a threat to our survival.

Sometimes there *is* a threat to our survival.

> One morning, whilst visiting family in Sri Lanka, I woke
> up to the sight of blood smeared across the tiles and
> splattered on the wall of the dining room.
>
> A huge snake had entered the house during
> the night. Apparently, this was not an uncommon
> experience in Sri Lanka. I can only imagine my Dad's
> reaction when he found a snake spreading itself across
> our dining room floor. Fear would have been the main
> emotion as there was a genuine threat to the safety
> of everyone in the house, most of whom were still
> sleeping.
>
> What followed was legendary.
>
> He gathered some of the neighbours and together,
> they managed to remove it. However, as the blood
> indicated, there was a struggle. Although my memory
> is hazy, it's possible that all of this occurred while my
> dad was wearing only a sarong and a singlet, which
> only adds to how legendary it was.

Very occasionally, we face a *real* snake. If this is the case, either run away
or get your neighbours together. More often than not, we are faced with
a snake *within*, which we *perceive* as real, although it's not.

The snake within us presents primarily in the form of *fear*:
- Fear of failure.
- Fear of judgement.

- Fear of rejection.
- Fear of the unknown.
- Fear of pain and discomfort.
- And even, fear of success.

It stops us from taking risks, starting new relationships, and pursuing our dreams. It prevents us from speaking in public, meeting new people and trying new things. Many of the best things in life are on the other side of fear.

Many of the best things in life are on the other side of fear.

It's not easy to face a snake, so what do we tend to do instead? We _avoid_ it. This can make things worse.

Meet Pei.

Pei was one of my patients. She had debilitating social anxiety.

It started small, with her skipping a few social gatherings with friends and avoiding people she didn't know at parties. She feared what others would think of her and worried they might find her uninteresting.

As time went on, her anxiety worsened. She began to struggle with interacting with her colleagues at work, avoided calls from clients, and ignored texts and calls from her friends.

Eventually, her anxiety became so severe that she couldn't even leave the house. She feared any form of social interaction. While there was no actual physical danger in these interactions, the intense and unpleasant feelings and thoughts generated by her anxiety made her want to escape them. Since social interactions triggered her anxiety, she began to avoid them altogether. The more she tried to avoid these distressing feelings, the more intense they became, and the worse her condition grew.

What if there is another way?

Pressure testing

The beauty of the Feel-Think-Do (FTD) model is that it demonstrates how feelings, thoughts, and actions are linked. The common sequencing is that feelings and thoughts *precede* our actions. Our actions, and therefore our results, are dictated by our feelings and thoughts. What if action *precedes* our feelings and thoughts?

Dr. Andrew Huberman, neuroscientist and host of the Huberman Lab podcast, once conducted an experiment on fear and courage using virtual reality. The simulation involved diving with great white sharks to evoke fear. David Goggins, a retired Navy SEAL, ultra-marathon runner, and former Guinness World Record holder for completing 4,030 pull-ups in 17 hours, is renowned for his philosophies on mastering the mind.

Huberman had the chance to put Goggins through this virtual reality experience. As Huberman explained the procedures, Goggins immediately mentioned, "I don't like sharks." Yet, when Huberman finished explaining and asked, "Who wants to go first?" Goggins was the first to raise his hand. Huberman later noted an important insight. Goggins had mastered the ability to use his behaviour to shift his perception, feelings, and thoughts — something most people usually try to do the other way around.

We can be our own biggest obstacle, feeling and thinking our way into indecision and inaction. The life that results from consistent indecision and inaction, is usually not one that is full, rich, and meaningful. In the previous chapter on *Flicking the channel*, we discussed how to shift what is happening "upstream" in our inside world, to radically transform what happens "downstream", in the outside world. The reality is that sometimes it is still not enough. When our thoughts and feelings are too strong, intense, ingrained, or intrusive, it can be difficult to change them, no matter how much we try to flick the channel.

> *Sometimes you can't think your way out of*
> *a problem you thought your way into.*

In such cases, we can still alter our perception, feelings, and thoughts, but we need a different strategy: *pressure testing*. This is a powerful form of psychological action that takes a reverse approach to what is conventional. Instead of addressing the inner world directly, *we focus on the outer world with the specific intention of influencing our inner world.*

The aim of pressure testing is to change our relationship with unpleasant feelings and thoughts. Instead of avoiding them, learning to embrace and even "chase" this discomfort will desensitise the impact they have on us. It is our relationship with unpleasant feelings and thoughts — usually one of avoidance — that is linked to our outdated survival instincts, that causes us to get in our own way. We become our own obstacle. Pressure testing teaches us how to get out of our own way by desensitising our natural aversion to fear. There is a metaphorical snake within us that we are trying to run away from. Pressure testing will allow you to become the snake charmer. Instead of running away from the snake, you play some music and coax the snake into coming out so you are face to face with the very thing that you are trying to run from. Over time, like a seasoned snake charmer, you can control the snake and make it sway and dance to your music instead of the other way around.

Don't run from the snake. Become the snake charmer.

What does this look like in practice?

Pressure testing involves creating environments that reproduce your uncomfortable feelings and negative thoughts, and then repeatedly and intentionally immersing yourself in these situations until it becomes easy. Does that sound crazy? Although it is hard and uncomfortable, it can be transformative and strangely addictive.

Pressure testing is about repeatedly and intentionally immersing yourself in environments that reproduce the discomfort you are avoiding, until it becomes easy.

The *pressure* is applied through repetitive and intentional immersion. This is what I call, "getting your reps (repetitions) in." In psychology, a similar process called systematic desensitisation is used to help people reduce their anxiety, stress, and avoidance through gradual and graded exposure to the source of their discomfort. Pressure testing is like systematic desensitisation on steroids. The results can be dramatic and accelerated.

Let's see how pressure testing set Jim free.

> Jim, 38 years old, had been on workcover for nearly four years after being bullied by his previous employer. This led to anxiety, insomnia and panic attacks, eventually preventing him from working at all. He was a great software engineer, but the fear of future bullying kept him from seeking a new job. Despite seeing multiple psychologists and trying a number of antidepressants, nothing was working.
>
> "I think you are focusing on the wrong thing," I posed.
>
> "What do you mean?"
>
> "The therapy and the antidepressants... what were you trying to change?"

"I was trying to feel better. I can't work when I am feeling so much anxiety. I have become so negative. I've been trying to work on all of my negative thinking because that has been holding me back."

"Yep. I think you have been focusing on the wrong thing."

"What should I focus on?"

"For years you have worked on trying to change your feelings and thoughts hoping that it would help you act differently, right?"

"I suppose. Yes, that's true."

"Why not focus on acting differently? You know that feelings, thoughts, and actions are linked. Your feelings and thoughts will eventually catch up."

I introduced him to pressure testing.

For the next two months we focussed solely on creating environments that reproduced his anxiety and panic. He was terrified of job applications and interviews. Bingo!

"Jim, when we pick an environment for pressure testing, it needs to have one very important characteristic: it needs to be safe. I know applying for jobs and attending interviews is scary, but it's safe. There is no actual physical danger. Do you agree?"

"Yes. It's scary, but that makes sense".

The next step was to apply the pressure. I encouraged Jim to repeatedly and intentionally immerse himself in this environment until it became easy. This meant job applications and mock interviews. A lot of them, in a short period of time.

"Jim, my prescription for you is simple. Get a job. That's it. You don't need more therapy. You don't need an antidepressant. You need to work and get paid for it."

"I know. But I am so scared that my future boss will bully me again."

"It's possible."

"Well, that's not helpful."

"No, it's actually very helpful. They may bully you. They may bully you even worse than at your previous job."

"What part of that is helpful?"

"Jim. I want you to get to a point where unless someone physically puts their hands on you, they can't hurt you."

"That sounds good."

"You have given these people too much power over you. I want you to go to your new job and be fine, even if they bully you. This is how you beat this."

"Wow. That would be great."

"Jim, life is hard. If it's not a bully at work, it will be someone or something else. Life doesn't get easier. You have to get stronger. Pressure testing will help you do that."

We boiled it down to simple mathematics. To get one job offer, he would need to do four interviews (a 25% success rate). To get one interview, he would need to submit ten job applications (a 10% success rate). In other words, he needed to submit 40 job applications to get four interviews, which would hopefully land him one job. Since it was hard to get an interview, we added that he needed to do a total of 20 mock interviews with family and friends to increase his chances of success.

I saw him a month later.

"This is hard. Pressure testing is making me super anxious."

"You were already anxious right? Let's get a reward from it. Otherwise, it serves no purpose."

"Haha, fair."

"Did you do the work?"

"Yes. So far I have done eight mock interviews. My sister in particular has been great. She even dressed up in a suit to make it all seem real. I also did 10 job applications."

He paused with a nervous smile on his face.

"I even got 1 job interview."

"Holy moly. Well done!" I said as I stood up to give Jim a huge high five.

"I am sure this has not been easy."

"Absolutely not Dr G. But, it's getting easier."

"What do you mean?"

"Well, I am less anxious overall. I guess I am 'getting my reps' as you say."

"Jim. Keep going. Just keep going."

He sees me four weeks later. With a big smile on his face.

"I have two job offers."

"Wait. Offers or interviews?"

"Offers," he replied with an even bigger smile on his face.

"WHAT?!?!?!"

"It worked. I did 20 mock interviews. I did 34 job applications and I have had three interviews already. I got two job offers. I am just trying to figure out which one to pick."

"Jim, I am so proud of you. I have to ask. Aren't you nervous about going back to work?"

"Yes. But that's fine. I know that unless someone puts their hands on me, no one can hurt me."

"What if your new boss is a bigger bully than the one you had?" I asked cheekily.

"Well, it's possible. Pressure testing has given me the confidence to face the snake inside of me. Worst-case, I can just find another job. It's not like I am scared of applying for jobs and doing interviews anymore!"

Jim was actually excited about getting back to work. He chose the job with a higher pay and the flexibility to pick up his daughter from school every day. He got off workcover, and I haven't seen him since.

How pressure testing changed my life

In high school, if the teacher asked a question, I would avoid eye contact and pray that they wouldn't pick me. Upon reflection, it was the *fear of failure* that kept me quiet. I feared saying something "stupid" so often I didn't say anything. This persisted throughout medical school. Once I was a doctor, I decided that enough was enough. It was time to confront the snake within. I used my fear as a trigger to lean into, rather than avoid. I raised my hand to answer questions, even if I didn't know the answer. I asked "stupid questions", sometimes in lecture theatres full of hundreds of my peers. I shared ideas to better help my patients, risking the possibility of rejection. Something amazing happened — the fear went away. A weight had been lifted off my shoulders. I felt free to express myself and developed a mantra: "Fail often and fail early." I was growing personally and professionally. Pressure testing helped me *get out of my own way*.

One of the most significant pressure tests of my life has centred around my scalp.

> Since I was 15 years old, I have been losing my hair. Self-conscious and fearing being ostracised for looking like an "old man," I tried various treatments: tablets, drops, and even a "laser hair cap". It worked! My hair grew back. One thing didn't come back though: my confidence.
>
> I hid my tablets. I prayed that no one would see my pillow cases, stained from the drops that I applied

to my scalp overnight. I was concerned that people would see me enter the clinic where I received my laser hair cap treatment. One day it hit me: although I wasn't losing my hair, I was still self-conscious.

I underwent an overnight pressure test. I went cold turkey and stopped all the treatment. That day, I went to a hairdresser and asked for it all to be cut off. The hairdresser asked several times if I was sure, and I was. When my wife got home, she almost fell over. I was still self-conscious but I had taken a big step forward. I was now looking the snake directly in the eyes. It was time to take it to the next level.

For the next few years, at social gatherings I would position myself below people's eye level. Why? I wanted them to see my baldness in all its glory. What gave me fear and anxiety was the thought of people seeing my bald spot. So, I decided to shove it in their face. At the start, I got teased, and in fact, I still get teased at times. Most of the time people don't care. My hair has continued to thin but my confidence has skyrocketed. I never needed more hair, I needed pressure testing. I needed to get out of my own way.

Over the years, pressure testing has really taken on a life of its own. As I alluded to previously, it can become strangely addictive. Here are some fun examples from my own life:

» I have spontaneously laid down in public (think restaurants, pavements) to get over my fear of other people's judgement.

» I have asked a flight attendant to give the safety announcement to get over my fear of rejection. They said "No".

» I have asked for discounts on things that I was buying to get over my fear of rejection and judgement. Interestingly, I have received a lot of discounts. $20 off a pair of shoes isn't that bad, right?

» I have gone door to door trying to sell a group fitness program to get over the fear and anxiety of putting myself out there. I literally had doors slammed in my face. I convinced two people to sign up and I made about $75 in those three months.

Pressure testing is exciting because it can set you free. Once you learn to get out of your own way, you can live a fully expressed, happy life that is full, rich, and meaningful. I've experienced incredible personal and professional growth thanks to pressure testing. While I'm thrilled with my progress, it saddens me to think about the growth I missed during all those years of letting fear dictate my actions. Keep in mind that the pressure testing never stops as there is always something you will fear. It's just that your threshold, what you can handle, will continue to rise.

"Life doesn't get easier or more forgiving,
we get stronger and more resilient."
~ Steve Maraboli

It's your turn

Pressure testing involves creating environments that reproduce your uncomfortable feelings and negative thoughts, and then repeatedly and intentionally immersing yourself in these situations until it becomes easy.

Step 1

Identify something that triggers an unpleasant feeling or negative thoughts. Choose a trigger that stops you from doing things you know deep down would be good for you.

Whatever it is, it will likely fall into one of the following categories:
- Fear of failure.
- Fear of judgement.
- Fear of rejection.
- Fear of the unknown.
- Fear of pain and discomfort.
- Fear of success.

Step 2

Create an environment that reproduces these unpleasant feelings and thoughts, whilst posing no *actual* danger. The environment needs to be *safe*. Aim to find an option that you can repeat easily.

Here are some examples:
- Public speaking.
- Asking for feedback.
- Asking for help.

- Lying down in the middle of the footpath for 30 seconds.
- Identifying a perceived vulnerability (e.g. bald spot) and exposing it publicly (e.g. sitting below eye level).
- Going door to door trying to sell something.
- Anything to do with sales.
- Asking strangers for money.
- Asking for discounts.
- Introducing yourself to strangers at parties.
- Starting a business.
- Standing up for yourself.
- Initiating difficult conversations.
- Trying new foods.
- Trying new experiences.
- Meeting new people.

Step 3

Repeatedly and intentionally immerse yourself in the environment.

Apply pressure and get your reps in:
- If it's public speaking, aim to speak in public 50 times in the next year.
- If it's asking for feedback, ask 10 family members, 10 friends and 10 work colleagues for feedback.
- If it's starting a business, spend the next 100 days building and selling your idea.
- If it's trying a new experience, Google "things to try", pick 10 things, and do them all.
- If it's lying down on the footpath, do it once a day for one minute at a time for 30 days in a row.

What to expect

The goal is to continue pressure testing until it becomes easy, meaning you no longer experience the same aversion to fear that drives you towards avoidance.

Pressure testing comes down to mathematics.

Quantity (i.e. amount of time doing it)

+

Intensity (i.e. how hard it feels)

+

Frequency (i.e. how often you do it)

=

Results

To the degree that you increase any or all of the variables of quantity, intensity, and frequency, you will experience better and faster results.

Quantity (i.e. time doing it) + Intensity (i.e. how hard it feels) + Frequency (i.e. how often you do it) = Results

Pressure testing with public speaking

Option 1:
- *Quantity*: 10 minute prepared speech
- *Intensity*: 4/10 in terms of discomfort as you are relatively comfortable giving short prepared speeches
- *Frequency*: Once a month

Option 2: Increase each of the variables
- *Quantity*: 30 minute partly prepared and partly unprepared speech
- *Intensity*: 9/10 in terms of discomfort as you are uncomfortable with not preparing all aspects of the speech
- *Frequency*: Once a week

Which would be more uncomfortable? Option 2.

Which would give you faster and better results? Option 2.

The more you do (quantity), the harder it feels (intensity) and the more often you do it (frequency), the better and faster your results.

The magic is in the *repetition.* Sometimes people push too hard too early and aren't willing to put themselves through it again. Find a level of discomfort that you are willing to repeat and immerse yourself in it.

Pressure testing starts with discomfort and ends with ease.

The relative ease that follows pressure testing will teach you that you *can* change your relationship with fear. The fear and anxiety that once caused you to run away can become the *reason* you do something. This is why pressure testing is a form of psychological action. Although the *work happens externally, the transformation is internal.* Don't forget that some of the best things in life are on the other side of fear. You will overcome outdated survival instincts and master the art of getting out of your own way. By doing so, you can pursue a full, rich, and meaningful life without limitations — a truly happy life.

Disclaimer: As I mentioned at the start of this book, some of the strategies in this book are not suitable for everyone. Pressure testing could be inappropriate for people with more severe mental health issues like post-traumatic stress disorder. Always consult with a medical professional.

Three rules

Pressure testing can become weird and wonderful. When you start asking to do the safety announcement on a flight or lying down in public places, you are officially experiencing the wild potential of pressure testing. It is only limited by your own creativity and the following three rules:

1. Whatever you do, it can't hurt you.
2. Whatever you do, it can't hurt anyone else.
3. Don't break the law.

Have fun, my friend.

Dr G's prescription

We can often be our own biggest obstacle to a life that is full, rich, and meaningful. Although uncomfortable, pressure testing helps shift your relationship with fear from avoidance to something that you embrace, allowing you to get out of your own way.

Turn to the corresponding page of your *Do Happy Workbook*, to complete the following exercise.

1. **Identify something that triggers an unpleasant feeling or negative thoughts.** Write down a few things that are holding you back in life.

2. **Create an environment that reproduces these unpleasant feelings and thoughts, whilst posing no *actual* danger.** If in doubt, pick something from this list:
   o Public speaking
   o Lying down in the middle of the footpath for 30 seconds
   o Identifying a perceived vulnerability (e.g. bald spot) and exposing it publicly (e.g. sitting below eye level)
   o Anything to do with sales
   o Asking strangers for money
   o Asking for discounts

o Introducing yourself to strangers at parties

o Trying new experiences

o Meeting new people

3. **Repeatedly and intentionally immerse yourself in the environment.**
    Apply pressure and get your reps in.

    Quantity (i.e. amount of time doing it) + Intensity (i.e. how hard it
    feels) + Frequency (i.e. how often you do it) = Results

    As you become more comfortable, apply more pressure by
    increasing the quantity, intensity, and frequency.

4. **Design a MAM. For example,**
    o Every time I feel fear, assuming there is no actual physical
       danger, I will lean into the very thing I am afraid of.

5. **Perform a 3650 forecast:**
    o 3650 X [Lean into fear on a regular basis] = Over 10 years,
       but likely much sooner, within weeks, your relationship with
       fear will shift. What you avoid will become the very thing you
       embrace. If life's most beautiful things exist on the other side of
       fear, imagine the life you will create with this small adjustment.

Chapter 19
Understand Control

"Give me the serenity to accept the things that I cannot change, the courage to change the things I can and the wisdom to know the difference."
~ Reinhold Niebuhr

Jane's family reunion took a dramatic turn.

"All of our family from across the world got together to celebrate my Grandfather's 90th birthday. It turned into a horror show."

"What happened, Jane?"

"My sister went out to get some milk from the shops. After an hour, she hadn't returned. My uncle came running through the door screaming, 'Come right now!' We ran about 300 metres up the road to find my sister lying unconscious on the pavement. My uncle started CPR and I called the ambulance."

"Jeez. That's heavy."

"She's currently in ICU in an induced coma."

"I'm so sorry."

"It looks like she got bit by a snake. They are not sure whether she will make it."

She continued, "Honestly, I'm a mess. Everyone is relying on me. I keep it together during the day because there are things that need to be done, I have to talk to the doctors and update the family. Even though she is in a coma, during the day I sit next to my sister and talk to her. At night, I'm overwhelmed with anxiety and panic. I can't sleep, and I'm starting to fall apart."

There are few things I know for sure about life:

- It is hard.
- It is unpredictable.
- It is uncertain.

In times of difficulty, understanding our relationship with control becomes critical. The less control we have over life, the more we need to focus on what we can control.

What can we control?

To understand control, all you need is a big square and a small square (see Figure 21).

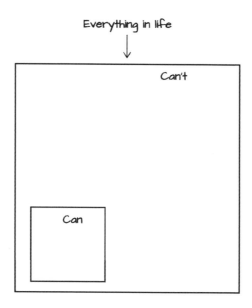

Figure 21

The big square represents *everything* in life. The small square represents what you *can* control. Everything outside of the small square represents what you *can't* control.

So, what can we control?

What we *do*. That's it. Period. Nothing else. Of course, our actions can take the form of the 3 P's: physical, psychological, and perspectival.

So, what can't we control?

Everything else. Everything other than what we do, we can't control (See Figure 22).

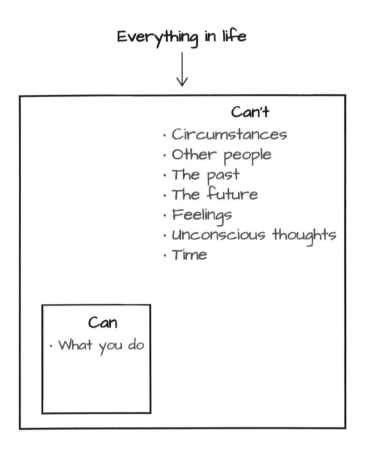

Figure 22

We can't control our circumstances. These are the facts, data, and events of life that occur and are out of our control. This could be as trivial as the weather or as significant as a life-threatening snake bite.

We can't control other people and their actions, thoughts, or feelings. We can hardly control ourselves.

We can't control the past. It has already happened.

We can't control the future. It is uncertain.

We can't control feelings. If that were possible, there wouldn't be a mental health epidemic.

We can't control the unconscious thoughts that form the running commentary in our head.

We can't control time. Time cannot be stopped, sped up, or turned back. It just marches on.

We can control what we do. We can't control everything else.

My work as a doctor has given me a crash course in the human condition and, over the years, I've witnessed a lot of pain and suffering:

» Being made redundant at work.
» Getting fired.
» Being bullied at work.
» Being assaulted at work.
» Being abused at home.
» Having a heart attack.
» Experiencing fallouts with friends.
» Being diagnosed with cancer.
» Getting old.
» Breakups.

» Committing suicide.

» Attempting suicide.

» Developing dementia.

» Losing a loved one, sometimes a child.

» Getting divorced.

» Losing all your savings on a bad investment.

» Having to live on government support schemes.

» Being homeless for years.

» Enduring chronic debilitating pain.

When life is slapping you in the face, something predictable occurs: *our focus insidiously shifts to what we can't control.*

Think of a time when you were struggling. Were you focusing on what you can control, what you can do, or everything else (e.g. the circumstances, other people)?

I am not sure why but there seems to be a natural human tendency to focus on the "can't" control part of life. This causes a lot of frustration which stems from *living in the "can't" control part of life, but thinking that we are in the "can" control part of life.* It is frustrating to believe that we can control something and yet have nothing to show for it.

Back to Jane.

> Jane's head was spinning.
> She was replaying the events (the past), struggling
> to grapple with their new reality (the circumstances),

and trying to shift from a state of debilitating fear, anxiety, and panic (feelings). All of this is in the "can't control" part of life which was making a very difficult situation even harder to deal with.

"Although this is not the first time I have heard of bad things happening to good people, it's always hard to watch people enter a storm with no certainty about when and how they will come out of it," I offered.

"It's the unknown that is getting to me. I am so frustrated about not being able to do anything about this, we just have to wait."

After offering Jane my love and support, I drew her two squares: a big one and a small one.

We documented all of her worries and placed them either in the "can" or "can't" part of life.

Everything she was worried about was in the "can't" control part of life:

- Whether her sister was going to recover (future and other people).
- If her sister recovers, whether she would be able to function in daily life (future and other people).
- Pleading, "Why? Why has this happened? Why now?" (Past, circumstances and other people).
- Her inability to sleep at night (circumstances).
- Feeling an overwhelming sense of anxiety and panic (feelings).

Then we examined what she can control. It turns out, plenty.

- Going to sleep an hour earlier.
- Starting the day with a walk outside.
- Coming to see her doctor (that's me!) regularly to check in.
- Seeing a psychologist to unpack and process the events.
- Avoiding alcohol or recreational drugs.
- Giving herself permission to rest.
- Checking in with her sister's doctors on a daily basis.
- Connecting with health professionals that she knows to help deconstruct the medical jargon and better understand her sister's situation.
- Prioritising the fundamentals — Exercise, Sleep, Nutrition, Relationships, Nature, Kindness, Gratitude, and Meditation.

We devised a long list of things she could control. She chose a few, such as going to bed an hour earlier, and committed to them. In the midst of tragedy, she began to intentionally focus her energy on the "can" control part of life.

I saw her a week later.

"What's the update?"

"She is still in an induced coma. It doesn't look good to be honest."

"Sorry to hear."

"I must say though. I am doing better."

"Why?"

"Most of this stuff is out of my control. I am just trying my best to live in the "can" control part of life. It is really helping. It's still horrible, but less so. I now have more mental space to actually focus on what's useful."

Can or can't?

Understanding what you can and can't control in life, and living in the "can" control part of life, is a big step towards taking full personal ownership of your happiness.

> "If you can control it, don't worry. If you can't control it, don't worry. Either way, don't worry."
> **~ His holiness the 14th Dalai Lama (paraphrased)**

Here are three steps to help you regain control of your life:
1. Ask, "Can or Can't?"
2. Ask, "What can I control?"
3. Pick the most useful answers and go *do* it.

Can or Can't?

If you are feeling distressed, ask yourself, "Can or Can't?". This will help you determine whether you are living in the "can" or "can't" control part of life. It will bring rapid awareness to your current situation and where you are placing your focus. My guess is that you will likely be focusing on what you can't control. Remember, if it is not something you can do, physically, psychologically, or perspectively, you can't control it.

What can I control?

Regardless of whether it's a "can" or a "can't", ask yourself, "What can I control?". Write down *as many* answers as possible. Aim for at least 10. Once you have 10, write 10 more. As we discussed in the *Flick the channel* chapter, "get to the corner of the whiteboard". The more options you have, the more control you have.

Pick the most useful answers and go do it

Assess your list of options, pick the most useful answers and go *do* it. Practise living exclusively in the "can" control part of life and you will notice something powerful: the scope of what you can control expands (See Figure 23). It's something that is hard to put into words and needs to be experienced to be believed. You will become increasingly resourceful, which is incredibly empowering. It contrasts sharply with the frustration and disempowerment of focusing on what we can't control.

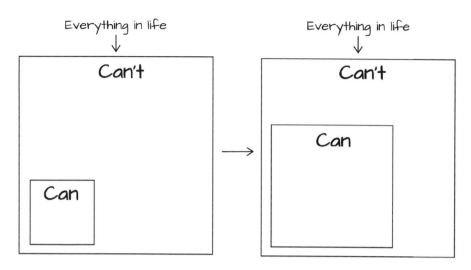

By focusing on what you can control,
you'll find you can control more.

Figure 23

Let's look at an example.

Situation: I have been made redundant at work. I am
feeling deflated and have a sense of injustice.

Can or Can't?
Can't.

Redundancy at work is a circumstance. I can't control it. I am feeling deflated and a sense of injustice. I can't control my feelings either.

What can I control?

An infinite number of things. Here are 20.

- Focus on the fundamentals — Exercise, Sleep, Nutrition, Relationships, Nature, Kindness, Gratitude, and Meditation.
- Reach out to my network to enquire about any opportunities.
- Update my resume.
- Upgrade my online presence through social media.
- Redefine my goals.
- Research new opportunities.
- Attend networking events.
- Consider freelance work.
- Invest in skill development.
- Seek feedback.
- Volunteer or intern to build my resume and stay active.
- Explore new industries.
- Audit my finances and create a budget to ensure financial security.

- Practise flicking the channel by asking, "What happened? What did I make it mean? Is it useful? What else can I make it mean?" (See the Flicking the channel chapter for more information.)
- Write down five things I am grateful for about being unemployed every day.
- Submit 50 job applications.
- Start a business.
- Seek mentorship.
- Take a break from work.
- Consider relocation for job opportunities.

Pick the most useful answers and go do it.

I would pick a handful of options that resonate with me and then focus on action. Personally, if I were made redundant anytime soon, I would start a business, but that's just me.

Dr G's prescription

Understanding what you can and can't control, and focusing exclusively on what you can control will make you increasingly resourceful in the face of life's difficulties.

Turn to the corresponding page of your *Do Happy Workbook*, to complete the following exercise.

1. **Write down a difficult or challenging situation in your life.**

2. **Follow the three steps to regain control:**
   a. Ask, "Can or Can't?"
   b. Regardless of the answer, ask "What can I control?" Write down at least 10 answers. The more options you have, the more control you have.
   c. Pick the most useful answers. Write them down. Now, it's time to commit to *action*.

3. **Design a MAM. For example,**
   o Every time I am distressed, I will ask myself, "Can or Can't?".

4. **Perform a 3650 forecast:**
   o 3650 X [Asking "Can or Can't?" on a regular basis] = After 10 years of shifting your focus to what you can control, the scope of what you can control will expand immeasurably.

Chapter 20

Lower Your Expectations

"Suffering is asking from life what it can't give you."
~ Ajahn Brahm

Abigail is the granddaughter of Roy Disney, co-founder of Walt Disney. This means that she is wealthy and knows many wealthy individuals. At an event hosted by the Patriotic Millionaires, she gave a powerful and emotional speech about how "billionaires are miserable, unhappy people." These are people who seemingly have everything — or at least the capacity to have everything — how are they miserable? Abigail describes jealousy as a problem, quoting issues like, "but his plane is bigger than mine... but he has more commas than I have." She also asserts that gluttony, the desire and pursuit of "more, more, more", is an affliction many billionaires face.

I don't write this to demean billionaires. I have never met one or talked to one. I am sure, or at least hope, there are many billionaires who are wealthy *and* happy. I present this to you to point out that *you can have everything and anything and still be unhappy.*

Compare this to the family I met in Vietnam.

> For a week, alongside a good friend, a small group of kind people from all over the world and local builders, we built a house for a low-income family. With support from Habitat for Humanity, one of the world's largest non-profit housing providers, we learned how to lay bricks and did so, one by one until we had a house to show for it.
>
> Every morning a small van would collect us from the hotel. We were dropped off at a local temple. We strolled along a winding path from the temple, passing barefoot children playing on the ground, fishermen preparing to catch food for the day, and people peacefully lounging in hammocks, until we reached the worksite.
>
> The family we were constructing the house for frequently visited to observe the progress. The house was modest, lacking any distinct features. Yet, there was something remarkable about this family — they exuded happiness. Their constant smiles, mirrored by their neighbours, left me pondering: how could they be happier than some of the world's wealthiest individuals?

A 2023 study of almost 3000 people from rural areas across 18 countries, including Kumbungu in Ghana, Laprak in Nepal and Vavatenina in Madagascar, showed similar findings to what I experienced in Vietnam. These people lived a subsistence lifestyle where their needs were met through fishing and farming. Modern day luxuries like smart phones and the internet were unheard of or, at least, unavailable. Despite having very little, these people reported life satisfaction ratings that were comparable to wealthy countries like Finland and Denmark, which are regularly deemed the "happiest countries in the world". It seems that once the basic needs of food, shelter, and safety are met, people are able to gain a great deal of satisfaction from the simple joys of life: going for walks, listening to music, socialising with family and friends, and spending time in nature. They have less, so they expect less.

Expectations and reality

Happiness, or unhappiness, can boil down to the relationship between two things:

1. Expectations
2. Reality

If you are happy, your reality will exceed or at least equal your expectations.

Happiness = Expectations ≤ Reality

If you are unhappy, your expectations will exceed your reality

Unhappiness = Expectations > Reality

Happiness is not a game of absolutes. It is a game of relativity. It is not about what you have, it is about what you expect relative to what you have. If you understand this, you can fast track your path to happiness.

> *Happiness is not about what you have,*
> *it is about what you expect relative to what you have.*

If you look at the happiness equation, you will realise that to become happier, you have two options:

1. Increase your reality
2. Lower your expectations

Let's explore both.

Increase your reality

This is the usual approach. The premise is that if you "increase your reality" by improving your circumstances, you will be happier.

Increasing your reality requires that you either get *more* or *better*.

You can always have more money, status, success and accolades.

You can always have better relationships, health, and lifestyle.

There are few traps with this approach. Firstly, your reality is a circumstance. If you recall from the previous chapter about *Understanding control,* circumstances are in the "can't" control part of life. If we are focusing on something we can't control, we are already starting to lose the happiness game. Secondly, happiness is not about absolutes. It doesn't matter what you have or how good it is, it only matters how it relates to your expectations. As our reality objectively improves, our expectations tend to slowly rise in proportion. We succumb to what I call *expectation creep.*

This often happens with our earnings. When you start working, your initial goal might be to earn $50,000 a year. Once you achieve that, you might aim for $100,000. After reaching that goal, you could set your sights on $200,000, $500,000 or even $1,000,000. It's not just your goals that are increasing, your expectations are also growing. Most people don't experience a significant increase in sustained happiness as their income grows. Perhaps it would be different if we made a billion dollars, right?

> *"Thanks to our capacity to adapt to ever greater fame and fortune, yesterday's luxuries can soon become today's necessities and tomorrow's relics."*
>
> **~ Richard Wiseman**

There's nothing wrong with improving our reality — more and better can be signs of growth. I'm also not advocating against setting goals. In fact, I love setting goals, sometimes big ones. We just have to be careful. While more and better may be a marker of improving performance, they don't necessarily equate to happiness. This is why, in the *Results as a compass* chapter, we discussed the importance of using our results as a compass to guide our behaviour, rather than an endpoint to reach. When it comes to happiness, *it is less about what you have and more about what you expect to have.*

Lower your expectations

The second option is to lower your expectations. It's counterintuitive and countercultural. From the day we are born, we are conditioned to value more and better. Society rewards us for increasing our reality, not for having low expectations. A common myth is that having low expectations will destine you to a life of mediocrity. However, you can lower your expectations and still live a full, rich, and meaningful life. It's not about lessening your life but rather, wisely placing your expectations. This will give you a sense of peace that no amount of "increasing your reality" can provide.

Expectations and control

You may have noticed that expectations are closely linked with control. As your level of control increases, so can your expectations. As your level of control decreases, your expectations need to be lowered.

Let's look at it through the lens of the "Can" and "Can't" control parts of life (See Figure 24) that we explored in the previous chapter on *Understanding* control.

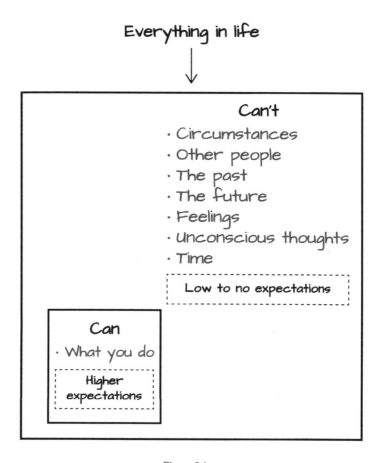

Figure 24

If you can control it (i.e. what you *do*), have higher expectations.

If you can't control it (i.e. everything other than what you do), have low to no expectations.

If in doubt, lower your expectations. You can never go wrong.

"Peace begins when expectations end."

~ Buddha

How to lower your expectations

Here are two ways to lower your expectations:
1. Become the fisherman
2. Prepare your mind for worst-case scenarios

Become the fisherman

The Fisherman's parable is a famous short story by Heinrich Böll that reminds us what it means to have enough. Beware, this parable has led many people to drastically change their life's goals and simplify their life.

THE FISHERMAN'S PARABLE

An American investment banker was taking a much-needed vacation in a small coastal Mexican village when a small boat with just one fisherman docked. The boat had several large, fresh fish in it. The American complimented the Mexican on the quality of his fish and asked how long it took to catch them.

The Mexican replied, "Only a little while."

The American then asked, "Why didn't you stay out longer and catch more fish?"

The Mexican said, "I have enough to support my family's immediate needs."

The American then asked, "But what do you do with the rest of your time?"

The Mexican fisherman said, "I sleep late, fish a little, play with my children, take siestas with my wife, Maria, and stroll into the village each evening where I sip wine, and play guitar with my amigos. I have a full and busy life."

The American scoffed, "I have an MBA from Harvard, and I can help you," he said.

"You should spend more time fishing, and with the proceeds, buy a bigger boat. With the proceeds from the bigger boat, you could buy several boats, and eventually you would have a fleet of fishing boats. Instead of selling your catch to a middle-man, you could sell directly to the processor, eventually opening up your own cannery. You could control the product, processing, and distribution," *he said.*

"Of course, you would need to leave this small coastal fishing village and move to Mexico City, then Los Angeles, and eventually to New York City, where you will run your expanding enterprise."

The Mexican fisherman asked, "But, how long will this all take?"

To which the American replied, "Oh, 15 to 20 years or so."

"But what then?" asked the Mexican.

The American laughed and said, "That's the best part. When the time is right, you can sell your company stock to the public and become very rich. You would make millions!"

"Millions — then what?"

The American said, "Then you could retire. Move to a small coastal fishing village where you could sleep late, fish a little, play with your kids, take siestas with your wife, and stroll to the village in the evenings where you could sip wine and play guitar with your amigos."

(Source: Likely adapted from Heinrich Böll's short story Anekdote zur Senkung der Arbeitsmoral which translates from German into "Anecdote on lowering work ethic".)

I won't add any further commentary to this parable because I don't want to take anything away from your own reflections.

Prepare your mind for worst-case scenarios

My favourite way to radically lower expectations is to *prepare my mind for a "worst-case scenario".* This is a fun and effective form of psychological action.

Here is an extreme example:

"Dude, are you human? Why aren't you stressed?"

My cousin posed this question to me just before we boarded an 18-hour trip from Japan to Melbourne. The flight wasn't the perceived problem. It was the three kids, all under the age of five, that we were travelling with.

"You really want to know?" I asked.

"Yes. Tell me."

"My expectations are really low. I am guaranteed to win."

"What do you mean?"

"I just have very low expectations for the flight. My mind is prepared for the absolute worst-case scenario. I am prepared for all the kids not to sleep. I am prepared for our whole group to have explosive diarrhoea from something we ate yesterday. I am prepared to clean the diarrhoea off the seats, the walls, and the roof of the plane. I am prepared for the other passengers glaring at us and scolding us for not being able to control the children. I am even prepared for a bird to get caught in the engine, or lightning to strike us, and for the plane to come crashing down. In this scenario, we might not even survive."

"Jeez, isn't that stressful?"

"You look more stressed than me."

"That's true."

"Here's the thing. Anything that is even a little bit better than what I just described would make me happy. Instead of all the kids being sick, maybe one of them is well. Maybe I only have to clean the diarrhoea off the seats and walls instead of the roof as well. Maybe the passengers glare at us but they don't say anything. Maybe a bird doesn't get caught in the engine and we don't get struck by lightning."

"You are weird."

"Hey, at least I'm happy."

Although preparing your mind for the worst-case scenario may seem grim, it is very effective in lowering your expectations. An added bonus is that its extreme nature can make it surprisingly fun. Given we are happy when reality exceeds our expectations, and most of the time the worse-case scenario doesn't happen, you are almost guaranteed to be happy.

Dr G's prescription

If you are happy, your reality will exceed or at least equal your expectations.

Happiness = Expectations ≤ Reality

Therefore, to be happier you can either increase your reality or lower your expectations. It's easier to lower your expectations.

Turn to the corresponding page of your *Do Happy Workbook*, to complete the following exercise.

1. **Write down a moment you were happy and reflect on the relationship between your reality and expectations.** Was one greater than the other?

2. **Write down a moment you were unhappy and reflect on the relationship between your reality and expectations.** Was one greater than the other?

3. **Design a MAM. For example,**
   o When you are considering adding more things to your plate, ask yourself, "What would the fisherman do?"

- o When are you unhappy, think of one thing that could be worse than what you are already experiencing. This is a form of "preparing your mind for the worst-case scenario".

4. **Perform a 3650 forecast:**
   - o 3650 X [Regularly asking, "What would the fisherman do?"] = A more intentional and simplified life over the next 10 years.
   - o 3650 X [Regularly thinking of one thing that could be worse in a given situation] = Over 10 years, this will lead to a greater appreciation of what you already have, rather than a growing desire to have more.

Chapter 21
Meditation for Awareness

"There is no good or bad meditation — there is simply awareness or non-awareness. To begin with, we get distracted a lot. Over time, we get distracted less. Be gentle with your approach, be patient with the mind, and be kind to yourself along the way."
~ Andy Puddicombe (Co founder of Headspace)

My first proper experience of meditation was during my fifth year of medical school. It did the opposite of what it was supposed to do.

In medical school, I had one sole obsession: passing my exams. I studied relentlessly but, admittedly, inefficiently. I would put in eight hours of work to get four hours of results. My self-care routines became non-existent. I went to sleep late and woke up early. I ate random things at random times. Sometimes I exercised. Sometimes I didn't. The outcome? To say that I was "stressed", which is what I would have said, was an understatement.

My mind was like a busy intersection in a capital city, racing with thoughts. I was anxious about what would be tested on the exams and whether I would fail. I desperately needed to relax so I did what most people think they should — I started meditating.

I had a very basic understanding of meditation at the time. I sat down, crossed my legs, and tried to focus on my breath for up to 30 minutes. I persisted for weeks. It was frustrating. I could hardly ever concentrate on my breath. Over time, I noticed that I was becoming more irritable in my daily life. Surprisingly, meditating seemed to make me more anxious.

It was only later that I realised meditation was teaching me two key things.

Firstly, I encountered the suffering that comes from personalising your internal world. Not only was I experiencing internal turmoil, *I became the turmoil*. This is probably why I was feeling worse. I didn't have the level of awareness required to separate myself from it.

Secondly, sitting in silence for that long, without any external distractions — no social media, no music, no one to talk to — forced me to confront the only thing left: *myself*. This was hard. It brought to the forefront what was already there: anxiety. To revisit the concepts from *Chapter 18: Get out of Your Own Way*, I was directly confronting the snake within. In this case, the pressure test wasn't something external but rather, something I needed to conquer internally. At the time, I wasn't ready for that challenge.

We will explore each of these in detail in this chapter.

Identifying with "me"

Our thoughts and feelings, especially the unpleasant ones, aren't inherently problematic. What matters is our relationship with them. When we personalise and become entangled in them, we engage in self-referential thinking. This type of thinking, which relates to having thoughts about ourselves, is crucial for self-preservation and survival. Without a sense of "self", we would lack the drive to survive or function in society. In essence, knowing your name, who you are, and what your favourite sports team is has its benefits. However, problems arise when we personalise events in our lives and get caught up in the drama of the outside and inside world. Technological advances and innovative research has allowed us to observe this in the brain, as it happens.

In *The Craving Mind*, psychiatrist and neuroscientist Dr Judson Brewer explains what happens in the brain during meditation. His research involved using functional MRI scans to observe brain activity in both experienced meditators and novices. Functional MRI allows researchers to see which parts of the brain are active during different tasks, a feat that would have seemed like witchcraft a few hundred years ago.

Surprisingly, Brewer's research found no increase in brain activity during meditation. Instead, they discovered *decreased* activity in the medial prefrontal cortex (MFC) and the posterior cingulate cortex (PCC). These areas are central to a network known as the default mode network (DMN), which is linked to self-referential thinking. Essentially, the DMN, and particularly the MFC and PCC, show increased activity when we think about ourselves or things related to us. Isn't it fascinating that these areas of the brain, known for self-referential thinking, decrease in activity during meditation?

When meditators, whether experienced or novice, reported feeling relaxed, there was a *real-time* decrease in MFC and PCC activity. Brewer noted that this decrease was most pronounced when participants weren't trying to achieve a particular goal but simply aimed to be present. For centuries, Eastern traditions have claimed that meditation dissolves the ego and loosens our attachments to the "self", thereby leading to a deeper sense of peace and happiness. Could this decrease in MFC and PCC activity be evidence of that phenomenon?

The less we identify with "me", the happier we become. This requires a subtle adjustment, and to understand it, we need to distinguish between the observer and the thinker.

The Observer vs the Thinker

In Eckhart Tolle's best-selling book, *The Power of Now*, he describes his initial personal struggles with depression and suicidal thoughts. With his will to die becoming stronger than his will to live, he was left with the incessant thought, "I cannot live with myself any longer". Despite his desperation, he noted a life-changing nuance in this statement. If there is an "I" and there is a "myself", does that mean there were two Eckhart's? Eckhart discovered that there is a part of us that "thinks" and a part that "observes" that thinking.

In the *Meditation for focus* chapter, we discussed the importance of cultivating our mind's ability to maintain single object focus. In this chapter, I will introduce meditation as a tool to cultivate *awareness*, by connecting with that which is observing the object itself. This can be referred to by many names: the mind, consciousness, the universe, or even God. I prefer the term "the observer", because it carries the least connotations in terms of religion, spirituality, or institutions. It simply describes what it does — it *observes*. The observer is the source of our awareness. As we connect from the perspective of the observer, we can use meditation to loosen the attachment we have to the thinking self, which is often mistaken for who we are.

The observer is the source of our awareness.

When we watch a movie, we may get engrossed in it, laughing and crying as if it were real. However, we know it's not real. The inner workings of our mind are a lot like this. The movie of our mind represents the *thinker*. The person watching the movie is the *observer*. The observer can still enjoy the movie but they are fully aware that they themselves are not part of it. There is a *big* difference between watching the movie and being the movie. When I was starting my meditation journey, most of the time *I was the movie*. I was connecting with and personalising the "thinker". This is why I was more irritable and anxious when I meditated — the blockbuster thriller of whether Dr G was going to pass his exams felt like the real thing. Imagine actually being one of the main characters in your favourite action movie. It would be stressful, right? I didn't realise that it was a movie that the thinker had constructed, one that I could have simply watched like any other award-winning film. I could have marvelled at the theatrics of my mind without personalising it and getting wrapped up in it.

> *The observer watches the movie. The thinker is the movie. There is a big difference between the two.*

The observer effect

The observer effect states that what we observe changes when we observe it. This seems to apply across many fields.

In physics, the observer effect is evident in quantum mechanics. The behaviour of particles appears to change when they are observed.

In psychology, the observer effect is noted when participants in a study change their behaviour when they know they are being observed.

In our minds, the "thinker" changes when it is being watched by the "observer". If you have 30 seconds, you can see this for yourself.

Here are some instructions from Eckhart Tolle:

Close your eyes and say to yourself, "I wonder what my next thought is going to be?"

Then become very alert and wait for the next thought. Be like a cat watching a mouse hole. What thought is going to come out of the mouse hole?"

What happened?

If you are like most people, you would have briefly encountered a silent mind—a mind momentarily free from any thoughts. In the *Meditation for focus* chapter, we explored the nature of a happy and unhappy mind. A wandering mind is an unhappy mind, while a quiet mind is a happy mind. I have meditated regularly for more than a decade, and one of my favourite discoveries is that when we connect with the observer, the thinker quietens down. Not only does connecting with the observer elevate our awareness of the present moment, it leads to a quieter and therefore, happier mind. The exciting part is that we *always* have access to this state.

Connect with the observer, and the thinker quietens down.

How to connect with the observer

Here are two ways to connect with the observer and build awareness:

1.   RAIN
2.   Clearing the mental inbox

RAIN

Meditation teacher Michelle McDonald developed the RAIN technique. It stands for Recognise, Accept, Investigate, and Non-identify. It is an active form of meditation where we can learn the mechanics of noticing and avoiding personalisation of what is happening in our life or mind. It is particularly useful if you often get stuck in incessant, intrusive, and obsessive thought patterns.

Recognise

Recognise what is happening in the moment by stepping into real-time awareness of your current state. This requires a "mental pause", where you become aware of the thoughts, feelings, or sensations that are arising within you.

Accept

Accept what is happening. This can be challenging. As I discussed in the *Get out of your own way* chapter, our survival circuitry makes us naturally inclined to resist unpleasant thoughts and feelings. Be aware of the subtle ways your mind might trick you into believing you are accepting something when you are actually trying to "accept it so it will go away", which is still a form of resistance. True acceptance involves allowing what is present to be there, and letting thoughts and feelings run their natural course without interference. Practice accepting both unpleasant and pleasant emotions and thoughts. This approach will prevent you from clinging to pleasant feelings like excitement or happiness, and resisting unpleasant ones like anger or fear. By doing so, you'll understand the essence of how awareness leads to acceptance — embracing things as they are without wishing to change them. Remember, the observer doesn't try to change the movie, it simply watches.

It may be useful to say something to yourself that encourages you to accept:
- "The door of my heart is open to you." (Inspired by Ajahn Brahm)
- "Let's ride this wave." (Inspired by Dr Judson Brewer and surfing in general)
- "Let's see what's in store."
- "Accept."
- "Allow."
- "Come in my friend."
- "Watch."

It doesn't matter what the phrase is, as long as the sentiment is one of acceptance and allowance rather than aversion and avoidance. I like to say such phrases with a gentle smile on my face, as I find this approach helps reinforce a sense of acceptance.

Investigate

Investigate what you are observing. Notice if your thoughts appear as audio, images, or videos. If you can hear your thoughts, do you recognize the voice? Is it your own? Where do you hear it coming from? If your thoughts come as images or videos, are they in colour or black and white? Are they large or small? Are you viewing them from a first-person perspective, through your own eyes, or from a third-person viewpoint? Pay attention to any feelings and physical sensations — are they pleasant, unpleasant, or neutral? Where in your body are you experiencing them? Are they changing?

Approach this process with the curiosity of a child, the compassion of a mother, and the kindness of a friend. Remember, we are not trying to change anything, but rather observe the nature of our inner world. The aim is to investigate and cultivate awareness of what we are observing. It's like watching a movie and investigating all the intricacies — the lighting, the camera angles, the characters' outfits, and the pitch and volume of the sounds coming through the speakers.

Non-identify

Non-identify by taking note of the investigation process, and recognising it as a separate entity that doesn't belong to you. This helps us to further connect with the observer, leading us to realise that we are not our feelings, thoughts, or physical sensations.

An effective way to do this is to label your experience:

- "I am feeling angry."
- "I will call this anxiety."

- "This is an angry thought."
- "This is fear."

The simple act of observing and labelling separates you from the experience, allowing you to become less caught up in it. The essence of the RAIN technique is to help us connect with the observer. As we shift from being the thinker to being the observer, the "hold" that an experience can have over us, whether it's perceived as positive or negative, will dissipate. This non-identification process prevents our identity from becoming entangled in the experience, allowing us to remain separate from it.

"You cannot be what you can observe"

~ Unknown

Here is an example of the RAIN process from my own life:

Context

In the midst of studying for my medical school exams, I begin feeling anxious.

Recognise

As soon as I realise that I am feeling anxious, I can begin the RAIN process. I can *recognise* and bring awareness to my current state of perceived anxiety.

Accept

With a smile on my face, I say to myself, "Let's see where this takes me." I notice my natural inclination to want this uncomfortable experience to stop and instead, focus on accepting it for what it is.

Investigate

Feelings and physical sensations: I observe a tingling in my chest, rapid shallow breathing, a heaviness in my head, and tension in the neck and shoulders. It is an unpleasant experience.

Thoughts: I observe recurring thoughts about what will be on the exams, whether I have studied enough, and what might happen if I fail. Most of these thoughts are in my own voice, but sometimes I see myself in the third person, sitting the exam and panicking as I run out of time to finish.

Non-identify

I say to myself, "This experience is what I would usually call anxiety."

For me, the RAIN technique allowed me to shine light on what I called "anxiety". I realised that it was an experience separate to me that I could objectively observe. It wasn't me. I wasn't my anxiety. There was never such a thing as "my" anxiety as it never belonged to me. In the same way that I would observe a stormy day outside as not belonging to me, I learned to observe a stormy day "inside" as not part of me as well. The hold that such intensely unpleasant emotions had over me dissipated, immediately. I hope the same for you.

I was not my anxiety and neither are you.

Now it's time to see what happens when you watch the movie all the way to the rolling credits. Introducing, the mental inbox.

Clearing the mental inbox

Email is the bane of my existence. I don't like it.

I have a passionate disgust for having an inbox full of unread messages. At the time of writing, I have 110 unread emails. It makes me want to cry. It also drives me closer to a future of living the life of a wandering monk (you think I am joking?). With this passionate disgust comes the occasional experience of pure bliss. It doesn't last long, but it is something special to behold. You guessed it. Once in a while, I muster up the courage and clear my inbox until it reaches *zero*.

However, there is something that bothers me even more than unread emails: the unread messages in my mind.

How many unread messages are there in your mental inbox?

How many thoughts do you have running through your mind at any given time? 10? 100? 1000?

It's nice to clear your emails but have you ever wondered how you can get your mental inbox to zero?

Do nothing

The art of doing absolutely nothing has been lost. We often fill our lives with noise, activity, and busyness, seeking distractions and external stimuli. As a result, whether intentionally or unintentionally, we lose the opportunity to face ourselves in silent solitude. Reflecting on my time leading up to my medical school exams, I found it distressing to sit alone. I suspect I was withdrawing from the addictive nature of being busy, while also resisting the discomfort of facing the turmoil within my inner world.

> *"All of humanity's problems stem from man's inability to sit quietly in a room alone"*
> **~ Blaise Pascal**

Pascal wrote this in the 1600s, suggesting that the discomfort of sitting in silence and being alone is a longstanding problem. This was long before the internet, smartphones, or hilarious memes. Perhaps there is an intrinsic need in humans to constantly be doing something. Yes, I understand the irony of writing a book called *Do Happy* that advocates unapologetically for action. Here, I am advocating for embracing the beauty of doing nothing, including the act of thinking. This represents a special form of psychological action.

How to clear your mental inbox

Sit down, close your eyes, and do absolutely nothing. It's okay to adjust your posture as needed to stay comfortable.

Aim to do this for a long time — 30 minutes is good; 60 minutes is great.

Practice consistently; daily for 3 months can be life-changing.

That's it.

Source: I would like to acknowledge Naval Ravikant for inspiring the concept of the "mental inbox".

As you can see, the process is very simple. It's not easy though.

The beauty of this meditation technique is that you don't have to do anything other than *watch* — just watch the movie of your inner world. If you want to go a step further, don't even do that. Just do nothing. By "nothing", I mean literally nothing: no scrolling on your phone, no watching TV, and no reading a book. Just you, sitting somewhere with your eyes closed in complete silence. If you think that this is a waste of time, you likely need this the most. It's a powerful exercise because you are left to confront the only thing that is left; *you.*

Just thinking about doing this might be stressful, which is a great insight worth reflecting on. Why is it so hard? Why can't we just do nothing for 30 minutes?

As our lives have become busier, it has become harder to do nothing. Thankfully, it's a skill that we can learn. The beauty of this meditation practice is that your mind will do *all the work*. It will naturally process all of your thoughts and "read the mail". All you have to do is allow it the time and space to do so. You will gain a deep understanding of the inner workings of your mind, your thoughts, and your feelings. It might be confronting — you may encounter messages you've avoided or suppressed, or painful memories from long ago that you had "archived". If you can put up with the discomfort, you don't have to do anything else. Everything else will unfold naturally.

Whether you are aware of it or not, this is your inner world. It is always running in the background, sometimes deep in the background. This practice will allow you to gain a level of awareness that few people experience. *It will be like turning on the light in a dark room.* The uncertainty of a dark room, your inner turmoil, will be replaced with the clarity of a lit room, inner peace. There will be a point at which your mental inbox will reach zero. If you thought clearing your actual emails gave you a thrill, this will be like nothing you have experienced. Expect a deep sense of peace, joy, and fulfilment. Needless to say, you will be happy. I promise. It will be like watching the movie till the rolling credits but instead of being left with a blank screen, you will be left with so much more.

Dr G's prescription

Meditation is a tool we can use to loosen our ties with the thinker and connect with the observer, the source of our awareness. As we become more aware, we learn to break free from the "hold" of our inner world and recognise ourselves as separate from it.

Turn to the corresponding page of your *Do Happy Workbook*, to complete the following exercise.

1.   **Make it RAIN**

Once a day for a week, write down when you experience a pleasant/unpleasant feeling or thought. Follow the RAIN process and document your reflections. This will help you learn how to non-identify with your experiences.

2.   **Clear your mental inbox**

Sit alone in a quiet room for at least 30 minutes a day, every day, for three months. As you can see, this will require some commitment. The rewards will be worth it.

3.   **Design a MAM. For example,**

o   Recognising each time you are experiencing a certain feeling (e.g. anxiety, sadness, worry, stress) and documenting it in a journal.

o   Sitting down, closing your eyes and doing nothing for one minute every day.

4. **Perform a 3650 forecast:**

    o 3650 X [Recognising each time you have a certain feeling] = Over 10 years, you can develop a heightened level of awareness not only of what you are experiencing, but also of the insight that you are separate from those experiences.

    o 3650 X [1 minute of doing nothing every day] = 3650 minutes (60.8 hours) of doing absolutely nothing after 10 years, an uncommon feat in today's society.

Part 4:

Advanced Skills — Perspectival Action

"Happiness is not found in external circumstances, but within my own perspective and mindset"
~ Unknown

In the *Do Happy* framework, there are three P's of action: Physical, Psychological, and Perspectival. Here, we will delve into the perspectival actions of happiness. These are more abstract and can be challenging to articulate. They can transcend language and at times, be "beyond concepts". They require experiential understanding. These fundamental shifts in your perspective can influence how you perceive the world, yourself, and happiness. The insights presented in the following chapters have the potential to be profound, transformative, and life-changing if you are open to receiving them.

Chapter 22

Death

"I'm not afraid of death. I just don't want to be around when it happens."

~ Dr G's nursing home resident

Death is lot like a driver and their car.

One Friday morning, I attended the nursing home to find out that Chester, one of my nursing home residents, had passed away an hour earlier. Chester and I had a lot of good chats. Sometimes I would be his doctor and talk to him about his medical problems. Most of the time, I would be like a long-lost grandson, listening as he shared his thoughts on politics, philosophy, and nature. I inevitably build bonds with many of my nursing home residents. After many years of working in nursing homes, I have also become used to letting go of those bonds.

When I found out that Chester had passed, I attended his room to offer my condolences to his family. It is always a surreal experience. I was speaking to Chester the week before about the news. This week, he was lying motionless in bed with his mouth open and eyes closed. Although his body was there, Chester wasn't.

It was as if the driver of a car had left their car behind.

When Chester died, two questions came to my mind:
1. Where did the "driver" go?
2. What makes for a good drive while we still have the car?

Where did the "driver" go?

Did he get another car? Like in rebirth.

Did he arrive? Perhaps in heaven. Chester wouldn't have belonged in hell.

Is he gone forever? A state of non-existence akin to what it was like before we were born.

What makes for a good drive while we still have the car?

We are all on the clock. It is important to reflect deeply and often about what is truly important. If you accidentally find yourself on a spiritual journey, like myself, many of these reflections will be not only about what is truly important but also, what is true. The inevitability of death is true.

I do about 5-10 death certificates a year. It is part and parcel of working in a nursing home. Over the years, I have seen many of my nursing home residents pass away. It didn't matter who they were or what they did, the driver just seemed to have left and they were not coming back. From housewives to war veterans, doctors to dentists, nurses to locksmiths, mothers, fathers and even a man who invented bomb detectors designed to save the lives of high-profile Australians in the Government. It is always humbling that the things we acquire and strive for during our lives, whether it's money, status, impact, or a family, are all left behind when we die.

A parable about death

Ajahn Brahm is a buddhist monk that has taught me more about the nature of life than anyone else.

This story about the nature of death is told by Ajahn Brahm in his book, *Opening the Door of Your Heart*.

FALLING LEAVES

Probably the hardest of deaths for us to accept is that of a child. On many occasions I have had the honour to conduct the funeral service for a small boy or girl, someone not long set out on their experience of life. My task is to help lead the distraught parents, and others as well, beyond the torment of guilt and through the obsessive demand for an answer to the question, "Why?"

I often relate the following parable, which was told to me in Thailand many years ago.

A simple forest monk was meditating alone in the jungle in a hut made of thatch. Late one evening, there was a very violent monsoon storm. The wind roared like a jet aircraft and heavy rain thrashed against his hut. As the night grew denser, the storm grew more savage.

First, branches could be heard being ripped off the trees. Then whole trees were uprooted by the force of the gale and came crashing to the ground with a sound as loud as the thunder.

The monk soon realised that his grass hut was no protection. If a tree fell on top of his hut, or even a big branch, it would break clean through the grass roof and crush him to death. He didn't sleep the whole night. Often during that night, he would hear huge forest giants smash their way to the ground and his heart would pound for a while.

In the hours before dawn, as so often happens, the storm disappeared. At first light, the monk ventured outside his grass hut to inspect the damage.

Many big branches, as well as two sizeable trees, had just missed his hut. He felt lucky to have survived. What suddenly took his attention, though, was not the many uprooted trees and fallen branches scattered on the ground, but the many leaves that now lay spread thickly on the forest floor.

As he expected, most of the leaves lying dead on the ground were old brown leaves, which had lived a full life. Among the brown leaves were many yellow leaves. There were several green leaves. And some of those green leaves were of such a fresh and rich green colour that he knew they could have only unfurled from the bud a few hours before. In that moment, the monk's heart understood the nature of death.

He wanted to test the truth of his insight so he gazed up to the branches of the trees. Sure enough, most of the leaves still left on the trees were young, healthy green ones, in the prime of their life. Yet, although many newborn green leaves lay dead on the ground, old bent and curled up brown leaves still clung on to the branches. The monk smiled; from that day on, the death of a child would never disconcert him.

When the storms of death blow through our families, they usually take the old ones, the "mottled brown leaves". They also take many middle-aged ones, like the yellow leaves of a tree. Young people die too, in the prime of their life, similar to the green leaves. And sometimes death rips from dear life a small number of young children, just as nature's storms rip off a small number of young shoots. This is the essential nature of death in our communities, as it is the essential nature of storms in a forest.

There is no one to blame and no one to lay guilt on for the death of a child. This is the nature of things. Who can blame the storm? And it helps us to answer the question of why some children die. The answer is the very same reason why a small number of young green leaves must fall in a storm.

*Ajahn Brahm's teachings are freely available online. If you are interested, find his guided meditation and talks here: **https://bswa.org/teachings/**

Doing Happy is about taking full personal ownership of our lives. To be happy *all the time*, you must take full ownership of *all of life*, including death. While finding happiness in good times is easy, finding it in difficult moments is challenging — and often where many answers lie.

Everyone who has ever lived, has or will eventually die — there are no exceptions. It is often said that "death and taxes" are certain, but not everyone pays taxes. Death is a natural part of life's algorithm. From the moment we are born, we sign a contract to one day die. Death is a scary and taboo subject for most people. However, finding a way to understand and accept this fundamental truth of life can be liberating. How you get there is a personal journey. It would be rude of me to take that gift from you. What I can do is share my own journey with you.

My perspectives on death (so far)

Perspectival action helps us reshape how we perceive the world and ourselves. When it comes to happiness, one of the most crucial perspectives we need to address is our view on death. As humans are designed for and driven by survival, there is a natural fear, resistance, and avoidance of death. This is very useful because, at the very least, it keeps us alive. However, it doesn't necessarily make us happier. In order to live a full, rich, and meaningful life, contemplating the role that death plays as a natural part of our lives is key. As you delve deeper into the fundamental nature of death, certain wisdoms will reveal themselves. It is likely obvious that I think about death more than the average person. Whilst this may seem morbid, it is hard to put into words the positive impact it has had on my happiness.

The following are some of the key perspectives I have adopted about death over the years.

The concert of life and death

This is another story from Ajahn Brahm. I often share this story with people who are dying, as well as with their grieving family and friends. They always find it helpful. I hope you do too.

As a young man I enjoyed music, all types of music, from rock to classical, jazz to folk. London was a fabulous city in which to grow up in the 1960s and early 1970s, especially when you loved music. I remember being at the very first nervous performance of the band Led Zeppelin at a small club in Soho. On another occasion, only a handful of us watched the then unknown Rod Stewart front a rock group in the upstairs room of a small pub in North London. I have so many precious memories of the music scene in London at that time.

At the end of most concerts I would shout "More! More!" along with many others. Usually, the band or orchestra would play on for a while. Eventually, though, they had to stop, pack up their gear and go home. And so did I. It seems to my memory that every evening when I walked home from the club, pub or concert hall, it was always raining. There is a special word to describe the dreary type of rain often found in London: drizzle. It always seemed to be drizzling, cold and gloomy as I left the concert halls. But even though I knew in my heart that I probably would never get to hear that band again, that they had left my life forever, never once did I feel sad or cry. As I walked out into the cold, damp darkness of the London night, the stirring music still echoed in my mind, "What magnificent music! What a powerful performance! How lucky I was to have been there at the time!" I never felt grief at the end of a great concert.

That is exactly how I felt after my own father's death. It was as if a great concert had finally come to an end. It was such a wonderful performance. I was, as it were, shouting loudly "More! More!" when it came close to the finale. My dear old dad did struggle hard to keep living a little longer for us. But the moment eventually came when he had to "pack up his gear and go home". When I walked out of the crematorium at Mortlake at the end of the service into the cold London drizzle — I remember the drizzle clearly — knowing in my heart that I would probably not get to be with him again, that he had left my life forever, I didn't feel sad; nor did I cry. What I felt in my heart was, "What a magnificent father! What a powerful inspiration his life was. How lucky I was to have been there at the time. How fortunate I was to have been his son." As I held my mother's hand on the long walk into the future, I felt the very same exhilaration as I had often felt at the end of one of the great concerts in my life. I wouldn't have missed that for the world. Thank you, Dad

Death can be beautiful

When I die, I want it to be the last thing left to try. The following are two stories about knowing when your time is up. It is not a time to resist, but rather a time to fully surrender to what lies ahead.

GWEN

Gwen was 96 and taking her final breaths. Her family was distraught. They knew the end was coming but it was still hard to let go. I sat with Gwen and asked her what she wanted. In her weak state, she muttered, "I just want to go meet my husband again." Soon after, she passed. I don't believe in an afterlife, but I sincerely hope I am wrong. As I write this, I hope that Gwen is going for a walk along the beach with her husband.

AN ELDERLY MAN

An elderly man once told me that he had "outlived his worth". He wasn't depressed or suicidal. It was his truth. He had lived a rich, full, and meaningful life. He was married for 60 years. His wife had died a few years earlier. He had a few kids. He got to meet his grandchildren. He built a small printing business and made plenty of money over the years. Death was the only thing left for him to try. He eventually did die.

When he did, it was beautiful. There was nothing left for him to do.

Death is neutral

I have learnt that for *every* bond I create with another person, whether that be with a loved one, a patient, or a stranger, I will eventually have to let it go. I have become progressively desensitised to the fear and grief of death. I now view it as a *neutral* event. Death is not good or bad, it just is. As we discussed in the *Flicking the channel* chapter, the circumstances are neutral and death is no different.

Death makes life precious

Regardless of what is happening in my life, every breath from now until the final one is a precious gift to be cherished.

I stepped into the meditation retreat and found a place to sit. At the front of the room, the monk began the session with a solemn declaration, "Today, we will contemplate death and our own mortality." This was going to be fun.

With gentle guidance, he led us through a profound meditation, inviting us to reflect on the impermanence that defines existence. We commenced by contemplating the vast expanse of time, acknowledging what had already risen and fallen. Ancient creatures, from dinosaurs to long-forgotten species, had all met the same fate. Then, we shifted our focus to humanity, recalling the countless souls who had born and died before us. From people we will never know to iconic figures like Gandhi, Einstein and Mother Teresa.

With sensitivity, the monk guided our thoughts to those we have loved and lost, evoking memories of departed family members, friends and acquaintances. As we pondered the inevitability of our own mortality, a sense of deep introspection replaced the room. In the depths of contemplation, I pondered the futility of life itself. Why invest in anything if our existence is destined to fade into obscurity? As the monk gently guided us back to the present moment, his words offered a valuable perspective. "You will one day draw your final breath," he reminded us. In that acknowledgement, he left us with this.

"You haven't taken your last breath yet, so it makes every breath until then precious".

The lowest expectation

If I die tomorrow, would I be okay with it?

I ask myself this question a lot. Over the years, my answer has definitively approached *yes*. This is not to say that I want to die — life is incredible and I love living. I simply accept that death is a part of life. Whether I die tomorrow or when I am a hundred years old, I can accept it. Of course, this is theoretical. I guess I will know for sure one day.

In the *Understanding control* and *Lower your expectations* chapters, we explored the relationship between control and expectations. At some point in all of our lives, despite our best efforts, death will be completely out of our control. If we can't control it, it is wise to have *no expectations*. There is no lower expectation than being ready to die. This is different from wanting to die, as wanting in itself is a desire that carries with it an expectation.

Only Now is certain

The past has happened and the future, other than death, is uncertain. All we can count on is right Now — the present moment. If every breath until the final one is precious, then being in the present moment allows us to soak in as many of them as possible. My understanding of what it means to be "present" is evolving. It is not simply a matter of being aware of what we are doing at a given time. Although that's helpful, there is a level of depth to the present moment, an almost infinite potential, that I am only starting to uncover. Perhaps this is something we can cover in a future book.

Insignificance, significance and non-existence

On a trip to Japan, I had a striking realisation: "There are so many people here — over 125 million." I felt insignificant. After I left, it struck me that one day I would die, and about 125 million people would never have known I even existed.

Contrast this with the relative handful of people I have direct relationships with. My wife, my parents, my brother, my nephews and nieces, my friends, my patients, my colleagues, and of course, myself. For these people, I am significant. I matter. They would care when I die. I also understand that in time they will move on, as I hope they would. Regardless, I will be forgotten in less than three generations. My kids will remember me. My grandchildren may remember me. Their children will be the last to have at least a fleeting memory or concept of "Gihan".

It's a notion that can feel both liberating and disheartening. The pursuit of a lasting legacy is often an attempt to defy the relentless march of time. Even the most illustrious names in history will eventually be forgotten. Once in a while, a historical figure such as Albert Einstein might be remembered for many generations. However, there will come a time where he is also forgotten, especially when you consider that despite most people thinking that Einstein lived many centuries ago, he only died in 1955!

It's an elegant balance between simultaneously being nobody for some, everybody for others, and eventually non-existent regardless.

Dr G's prescription

Everyone — those you care about, those you don't care about, those you've never met, and you yourself — will eventually die. To be happy *all the time*, you need to accept *all of life*, including death.

Turn to the corresponding page of your *Do Happy Workbook*, to complete the following exercise.

1.   **If you are open to it, write your own eulogy.**
This will be a useful way to directly contemplate your own death.

2.   **Answer and re-answer questions such as the following:**
   a.   What is death?
   b.   What happens after you die?
   c.   What makes for a good life?
   d.   If I die tomorrow, would I be okay with it?
   e.   Am I ready to die soon?
   f.   What would I focus on if I knew I was going to die in 12 months?
   g.   When I die, what could be some of my regrets? How can I prevent this?

Happy driving my friend.

Chapter 23

Unconditional Happiness

"Most people ask for happiness on condition.
Happiness can only be felt if you don't set any condition."
~ Arthur Rubinstein

Is your happiness conditional?

In 2013, during a demanding research year, I found myself curled up in a ball and crying. My girlfriend (now wife) was trying her best to console me.

"I am sick of this. I keep getting told that once something happens, then I will be happy. It's just not true! First it was getting into Medicine. I thought that if I work hard and get into Medicine, then I will be happy. Medicine is harder than school! Then it was research. If I do some good research and get it published, then I can get a really good job and be happy. Now it is to become a doctor. If I finish medical school and

become a doctor, then I can be happy, right? It's all a
lie. It's not true!"

I was met with a painful realisation.

Conditional happiness is a loser's game.

I had trained myself to believe that if I met certain conditions in my
life, then I will be happy. It wasn't the case. There is another subtle
undertone in my story. I had also convinced myself that happiness
cannot exist in the presence of pain, adversity, and suffering. Given
that life by its very nature is hard, these conditions for happiness were
unrealistic and unachievable.

I was met with another painful realisation.

Conditional unhappiness is also a loser's game.

If-then-else

Happiness is a lot like coding. Programming languages, like Python
(not a snake), use "if-then-else" statements to execute certain code if
specified conditions are true.

For example, you can write a piece of code to check if someone needs
cheering up.

```python
# Define happiness level
my_happiness_level = 3

# Check if I need cheering up
if my_happiness_level < 5:
    print("I'm feeling a bit down. I could use some cheering up!")
else:
    print("I'm feeling pretty good right now.")
```

Source: Generated using ChatGPT

In other words:

» *If* condition (i.e. happiness level is <5) is met, *then* outcome (print — "I'm feeling a bit down, I could use some cheering up!").

» *If* condition is *not* met (i.e. happiness level 5 or more), *else* outcome (print — "I'm feeling pretty good right now.").

If we look at conditional happiness like a piece of code, it may look like this.

» *If* condition (insert favourable circumstance), *then* happy.

» *If* condition (insert favourable circumstance) not met, *else* unhappy.

If we look at conditional unhappiness like a piece of code, it may look like this:

» *If* condition (insert unfavourable circumstance), *then* unhappy.
» *If* condition (insert unfavourable circumstance) not met, *else* happy.

We often believe that if something happens or changes, then we will be happy. As soon as we have conditions like this, you sign a contract to be unhappy until these conditions are met.

» *If* [find partner], *then* [happy].
» *If* [finish project], *then* [happy].
» *If* [make more moncy], *then* [happy].
» *If* [get promotion], *then* [happy].
» *If* [good weather], *then* [happy].
» *If* [financially secure], *then* [happy].
» *If* [become a doctor], *then* [happy].

We also believe that if there is pain, adversity, and suffering, then we can't be happy. Until there is relief from such circumstances, we sign a contract to be unhappy.

» *If* [criticised at work], *then* [unhappy].
» *If* [get sick], *then* [unhappy].
» *If* [break up with partner], *then* [unhappy].
» *If* [made redundant at work], *then* [unhappy].
» *If* [lose money], *then* [unhappy].
» *If* [lose loved one], *then* [unhappy].

Put simply,

» Conditional happiness = *If* [insert favourable condition], *then* happy
» Conditional unhappiness = *If* [insert unfavourable condition], *then* unhappy

Believing that happiness, whatever that means to you, is conditional to something happening (i.e. good stuff) or not happening (i.e. bad stuff) is flawed. It is a guaranteed way to lose the game of happiness.

The destination is boring

Charlotte was a patient of mine. She was moving houses and struggling with severe anxiety.

"I am super anxious," she said.

"Tell me more."

"I have had anxiety for most of my life. I am moving houses and it's really getting to me. I have lived in this house for 30 years. I am leaving behind a lot of great memories. It's making me very anxious."

"You said that you were anxious for most of your life?"

"True. But it's worse these days because we are moving houses."

"Some studies have shown that people would rather get a colonoscopy without sedation than move houses."

"Really?"

"Haha, I am just joking. It's a hard thing to research because it wouldn't pass the ethics approval process."

"Anyway, after the move I should be OK."

"Really? Didn't you say you have been anxious for most of your life?"

"Yes, but if I get through this, then I can relax and be happy."

"I don't agree."

"What?"

"It won't be OK after the move. Something else will take its place."

"Jeez thanks."

"Think about it. You were anxious before the move. You are anxious during the move. Why wouldn't you be anxious after the move?"

"So do I need an antidepressant or a sedative or something?"

"No no! That's not what I am trying to say. Can't you see what's happening here?

"What?"

"The anxiety you describe, paints a picture of a better future. However, when the future arrives and becomes your present, it re-paints a picture of a better future again. You can't win this game."

"Wow! That's so true. In fact, after I move houses,
I have to help my son organise his wedding. I am
actually quite anxious about that as well."

Charlotte had created conditions for her happiness that were never going to be met. The cure for her unhappiness was independent of what happened in the future. If only Charlotte heard the speech my older brother gave at my wedding. He famously said, "the destination is boring". We often believe that reaching a goal — whether it's a job promotion, a dream home, financial freedom, finding love, or moving to a new place — will make us happy and solve our problems. The destination becomes the condition that we believe we need to meet to be happier. But once we reach that destination, we *immediately* start looking for the next one. It is a cycle that doesn't end. We need a better way.

Ask great questions

As Carl Jung put it: "To ask the right question is already half the solution to a problem."

Once I became aware of the conditional nature of my happiness, I couldn't unsee it. I was obsessed with what it would take to be happy *all the time*. Once I realised that conditional happiness couldn't give me this, I started to ask better questions.

As I mentioned in an earlier chapter, this is the question that changed my life.

How can I be happy before, during and after anything?

Put simply,

How can I be happy <u>all</u> the time?

This led to a whole host of follow up questions.

» What conditions need to be met for sustainable lifelong happiness?
» Is there a form of happiness that is unconditional?
» What would need to be true for me to be happy all the time?
» If I was happy all the time, would that mean happiness can't be a feeling because feelings are transient?
» Biriyani makes me happy. Should I just eat biriyani all the time?

After years of self-enquiry, research, and experimentation, I learnt that for these questions to be answered, it required a significant shift in *perspective*. In previous chapters, I explained the power of psychological action to change our thinking and therefore our actions and results. The perspectival actions I introduce in this chapter serve more as changes in mindset that sit "behind" our thoughts and influence how we fundamentally experience the conditions of life, irrespective of what they are. It can lead to a much deeper form of fullness, richness, and meaning in our lives, rooted in wisdom and understanding.

Despite spending a significant part of my adult life exploring these concepts, I *still* succumb to conditional forms of happiness and unhappiness. Trust me, no one is more disappointed than me.

Here are some personal examples that hold true for me at the time of writing.

» *If* [publish book], *then* happy.
» *If* [sell 1000 copies], *then* happy.
» *If* [run 5km in 20 minutes], *then* happy.
» *If* [one date a week with wife], *then* happy.
» *If* [unhealthy], *then* unhappy.
» *If* [poor sleep], *then* unhappy.
» *If* [eat sugary foods], *then* unhappy.
» *If* [lose money], *then* unhappy.

If these conditions are not met, then I am happy.

Nevertheless, I understand that if I am unhappy, it's not because a condition has or hasn't been met. The issue lies in the very nature of setting conditions for our happiness.

Practising unconditionality

The following three perspectives have been an invaluable source of strength for both me and the people I work with. They can help us move beyond conditions and progress towards a more unconditional form of happiness.

1. Getting to have a bad day
2. Turning pain into purpose
3. Happiness for no reason

Getting to have a bad day

Conditional forms of happiness require that we either attain favourable conditions or relief from unfavourable conditions. Winning the happiness game requires that you design these conditions in a way that you can't lose. If you can be happy when you are sick, exhausted, been fired from work, lose a lot of money, receive a scary diagnosis, or someone you love dies, you will always win. If you can find a way to be happy in these conditions, what's left? This requires a ruthless lowering of expectations. As I discussed in the previous chapter on *Death*, the lowest expectation is to be ready for death. As morbid as it sounds, part of me doesn't even expect to wake up in the morning. For the time being, I have been waking up. It is always a pleasant surprise.

The equation now looks like this.

If I wake up in the morning, then happy.

If I wake up today, that means I get to live life for at least a bit longer. This makes me incredibly happy. Even on a really "bad" day, I am still happy because I *get* to have a bad day. The alternative is not waking up, which one day will be the case. By adjusting your perspective in this way, you can find happiness even on your bad days.

Turning pain into purpose

Life is hard. Everyone, without exception, will experience pain, adversity, and sickness in their lifetime. Life will slap us in the face whether we like it or not. Some people get slapped harder than others but, nonetheless, everyone gets their turn.

It is easy to conceptualise happiness when things are going well. It is much harder when things are not going well. When things go well, they become a condition for your happiness. Conversely, when things don't go well, they become a condition for your unhappiness.

When I reflect on the difficult periods of my life, I realise that they have shaped me into the person I am today. If given the opportunity to change anything about my past circumstances, I wouldn't. I wouldn't change being bullied. I wouldn't change the severe anxiety I went through in medical school. I wouldn't change the hundreds of "no's" I have received in business. I wouldn't change all the issues with friends and family I have had over the years. Many of these painful experiences have given me purpose in later stages of my life.

Think of something that you have overcome in your life. If you could go back in time and change it, would you?

Most people, for most things, say "No". Why?

Pain, adversity, and suffering, given enough time, can help us become better versions of ourselves. *Do Happy* is a testament to this. Without enduring periods of unhappiness, there would be no *Do Happy*. My own suffering gave me a sense of purpose and a drive to assist others struggling with similar issues. I feel a deep obligation to help the person I once was.

If you have ever worked with me, you would know that my response to one's suffering is counterintuitive. When a patient or client tells me about something "bad" that has happened, if it's appropriate, I muster up as much compassion as I possibly can and respond with the words:

"That's great news!"

A perspective that today's pain will become tomorrow's purpose makes the pain in some ways, beautiful. It requires time and faith.

Today's pain will become tomorrow's purpose.

I am reminded of John Lennon's famous quote, "It will all be okay in the end. If it's not okay, it's not the end."

Can you adopt such a perspective *during* the storm?

It is easier to reflect on the purpose of a difficult period after it has happened. Can you embrace this purpose *in real time*, in the midst of hardship? It's not easy but it's a powerful form of perspectival action that will allow you to find happiness, even in the darkest of times. When I face tough times now, I remind myself, "It's great news," because I know it will eventually provide a sense of purpose. Overcoming these challenges allows me to help others do the same. Purpose is when you recognise that working through your pain now can help someone else relieve theirs later.

Here's a story from one of the most inspirational people I have coached. She had been through some traumas in her life and wanted help to move on.

> "After nearly two years of working together, what do you think this has all been about my friend?" I asked as a proud coach.
>
> "It's been about getting over my own sh**. I just don't want to feel broken anymore."
>
> "What do you mean?"
>
> "If I can stop feeling broken, everything in my life will change."
>
> "Why?"
>
> "I'm not sure. I just want to be able to tell my story so that I can help other people."
>
> "Why?"
>
> "It feels like winning."
>
> "Why?"

"I can't explain it."

"Try."

"Because then I won't feel so broken. Then what happened wouldn't have been for nothing. The pain would have a purpose."

"You have been practising your ability to speak and tell your story for months now. You have done hours of 'reps'." (Yes, she underwent pressure testing.)

"Yes."

"When you have told your story, do you think it has helped anyone?"

"Now that you mention it, yes. I have had a lot of people tell me that it was inspiring and gave them hope."

"Your story is already helping other people my friend."

"Wow, yes."

"Doesn't that mean you are already winning?"

After a long pause...

"Wow, yes."

"Are you still broken then?"

After a longer pause...

"No."

"Have you ever said that out loud before?"

"No."

"Remember when you said that if you can stop feeling broken, everything in your life will change?"

"Yes?"

"Welcome to your new life."

She becomes speechless, looking around with a big smile on her face as if she was seeing the world for the first time.

"I am so sorry that I am the first person you have to see," I said half-jokingly.

"Are you religious?" I asked.

"No."

"Neither am I. However, I want to tell you a story. Rory Vaden is one of my favourite entrepreneurs and a man of faith. He believes that our pain has a purpose. Once you move through your pain, you are better for it. Not only that, he believes that the burning desire that you have to help other people is a signal. That signal doesn't come from you. It comes from someone else. That someone else is literally on their hands and knees praying for you to help them because only you can."

Still speechless.

"Here's the thing. I love to help people. For some people, I am very good at helping them. For a handful, I may be the best person in the world to help them. There are people out in the world that are waiting for you to help them. Everything you have gone through makes you perfectly positioned to do so."

She remained speechless, soaking in a new perspective on life.

"I am so proud of you."

Happiness for no reason

Many of the conditions we have for our happiness exist in the future. The future is uncertain. If you don't believe me, ask the farmer.

WE'LL SEE

Once upon a time, there was an old farmer.

One day his horse ran away. Upon hearing the news, his neighbours came to visit. "Such bad luck," they said sympathetically, "you must be so sad."

"We'll see," the farmer replied.

The next morning the horse returned, bringing with it two other wild horses.

"How wonderful," the neighbours exclaimed! "Not only did your horse return, but you received two more. What great fortune you have!"

"We'll see," answered the farmer.

The following day, his son tried to ride one of the untamed horses, was thrown, and broke his leg. The neighbours again came to offer their sympathy on his misfortune. "Now your son cannot help you with your farming," they said. "What terrible luck you have!"

"We'll see," replied the old farmer.

The following week, military officials came to the village to conscript young men into the army. Seeing that the son's leg was broken, they passed him by. The neighbours congratulated the farmer on how well things had turned out. "Such great news. You must be so happy!"

The man smiled to himself and said once again. "We'll see."

This parable illustrates the fallacy of jumping to conclusions or labelling events as strictly good or bad because future outcomes are uncertain. If we are to find a way to be happy all the time, it can't rely on uncertainty. Therefore, what happens in the future cannot be a necessary condition for our happiness.

Alternatively, what if your happiness required *no conditions*. If there are no conditions for your happiness, you can be happy for no reason.

> *If there are no conditions for your happiness,*
> *you can be happy for no reason.*

Happiness can be unconditional. What is truly without conditions? *The present moment.*

What is happening Now has no conditions; it just is. A convenient and valuable truth is that connecting with the present moment often brings a sense of peace, joy, and happiness. The physical body is always present — it cannot be in the past or the future, it is always exactly where it is. The mind, however, has a tendency to wander. This comes at a cost to our peace and happiness. If you are able to train your mind to be present, it can learn to be happy with no more than what is already there. In other words, you can learn to be happy for no reason.

Unconditional happiness = If [any condition], then happy.

If you want to be happy all the time, the traditional model of conditional happiness doesn't work. You can either change the conditions so you can't lose (i.e. getting to have a bad day), view pain as a pathway to purpose (i.e. turn pain into purpose), or move towards an unconditional model form of happiness (i.e. happiness for no reason). The latter option we will explore more in the next and final chapter, *Meditation for wisdom*.

Dr G's prescription

Conditional happiness, and unhappiness, is a loser's game. Approach a form of happiness that is unconditional, and you can be happy all the time.

Turn to the corresponding page of your *Do Happy Workbook*, to complete the following exercise.

1. **Write down your current conditions for happiness — what do you think you need to be happy?**

2. **Write down your reflections on how you can reduce, or even remove, these conditions.**

Chapter 24

Meditation for Wisdom

"Silence isn't empty, it's full of answers."
~ Unknown

Perhaps the most powerful perspectival action you can take comes from answering the question, "Who am I?" The answer may lead you to an unconventional perspective, but one that can offer a form of happiness that you can always access.

Who am I?

It was our last session after six months of working together. It was a powerful one.

> "For a while now, I have been asking myself the question, 'Who am I?'"

"That sounds about right for you Dr G," he replied with a cheeky smile on his face.

"Well, let me ask the question on your behalf. Who are you?"

Pausing to ponder the seemingly simple question, he responded.

"I am James. I am an accountant. I run my own business. I am a brother, a son, a grandson, a boyfriend, and a friend. I am a kind and caring person that wants to make a difference in the world."

"I am so glad I asked. That's beautiful. If I take away your name, are you still you?"

"Yes, I am still me. It's just a name."

"Ok, let's take away your accountant title. Oh, and you no longer run a business. What's left? Are you still you?"

"Yes. I am still me. Work doesn't make me who I am."

"Ok, let's say you are no longer a brother, a son, a grandson, or a friend. You have no recollection of this. Now what's left? Are you still you?"

James started to become a bit nervous.

"I don't think I will be me anymore. Those things are important. They make me who I am."

"Let's keep going. What if you didn't have a past anymore? You are just a guy that's sitting there. All of the stuff that happened from the day you were conceived till right now, are erased. Are you still you?"

"I don't know. A man with no past. I would be like a ghost."

"Okay now, you have no future either. No dreams. No plans. You are just a guy that's sitting there, with no past and no concept of a future. Are you still you?"

"No, I don't think so."

"What's left?"

"Maybe my values? I think I would still be kind. That's something that just comes from deep within me."

"Ok, let's strip away your values as well. Are you still you?"

"Definitely not."

"What's left?"

"Maybe my body? Like my five senses?"

"Let's imagine for a moment that we've stripped away your five senses. You no longer have the ability to see, hear, feel, taste, or smell."

With a smile on my face, I inquire, "So my friend, what's left?"

"Jeez. Maybe my thoughts and feelings."

"Ok. Let's strip away your thoughts and feelings too. What's left now?"

After a long pause, a look of disbelief, awe, and slight fear simultaneously appeared on his face.

"I think it's *me*."

He continued: "I feel like I am going to cry. I don't know why. That's scary."

The traditional concept of who we are, our identity, is constructed. It has building blocks. It is made up of our job titles, the roles we play in life, the people in our life, our past, our future, our body and its senses, our values, our feelings and our thoughts. Once you strip away all of these layers, you are left with one thing, nothing. Except for the observer of that nothing.

If you follow the process of stripping away all the layers of identity for anyone: whether it's Dr G, a loved one, a celebrity, an animal, your enemy, or even people who have committed horrible acts (e.g. abuse, murder), you will end up at the same place, the observer.

"So what?" James asked curiously.

"It means that we are all fundamentally the same," I responded.

Many of us need validation to confirm our sense of self-worth. We seek approval through external validation, needing approval and recognition from others. Pressure testing is a great way to reduce our need for external validation. Then, we can move away from seeking external validation and cultivate it internally. Gratitude journaling, particularly focusing on self-gratitude, will validate your worth from the inside out. If you stop here, you can lead an extraordinary life. However, there is another level — a state where we require *no validation*.

"What do you mean 'no validation' Dr G?"

"When you strip away all of the layers and come to the conclusion that we are all fundamentally the same, it leads to what I call a 'deep knowing.'"

"You lost me."

"A deep knowing stems from the realisation that we are all the same. If we are all the same, then as a default, you, me and everyone else is worthy of love, joy, peace and happiness."

Something clicked for James.

"Wow. I feel like crying. Then I feel light. Then I feel like crying again. There is so much compassion in that for yourself and everyone else. We are all the same. Ahhh, I feel like the pressure has been lifted."

To fully answer the question, "Who am I?", we need to *let go* of our constructed layers of identity. Once you do this, what's left? It should be nothing, an "empty" experience. Paradoxically, it is a very full experience, as James was able to glimpse.

Constructing an identity

Our perception of who we are, what we consider our identity, is continually shaped from the day we are conceived. If we consider our identity as constructed, with layers that are prone to change, we can start to explore an alternative perspective of who we truly are.

To help you understand this concept, let's explore the following 12 layers of identity.

1. The past
2. The future
3. Roles and responsibilities
4. Relationships
5. Cultural and geographical upbringing
6. Family upbringing
7. Education
8. Religion and spirituality
9. Socioeconomic status
10. Beliefs, attitudes and values
11. The five senses and our body
12. Thoughts and feelings

The past

Everything that has happened from the day you were conceived until right now as you are reading this, can influence your identity. What happens in the past — and in particular how we relate to it — has a dramatic impact on our identity. As you have probably noticed, as time passes, the meaning you attach to past events *naturally changes*. This means that the idea of "you", will also evolve over time. In other words, identity is not fixed, it's fluid.

When I was in high school, I got bullied for having big ears. They used to call me "Dumbo the elephant"! In retrospect, it was kind of funny. During those years of my life, my appearance was a big part of my sense of identity and those words hurt.

Decades later, I am very grateful for that period in my life because it set me on a path to discover how to be happy and help others find happiness as well. Now, I identify as "Dr G" or the "happy guy", someone who absolutely loves his big ears.

Over time, how I relate to past events such as this has changed, and with it, so has my identity.

The future

Our intentions, plans, goals, and dreams for the future also play a crucial role in shaping our identity. Whether it's your career aspirations, where you want to live, or whether you wish to get married and have children, all of these factors contribute to defining who you are.

I asked my 6-year-old niece, "What do you want to be when you grow up?"

She answered enthusiastically, "I want to be a scientist, a doctor, a teacher, an astronaut, and a dancer!"

I asked my 10-year-old nephew the same question.

He answered, "I want to be a builder. I want to build couches so that when I get tired, I can sleep on them."

You can immediately learn something about my niece and nephew and the type of people they are.

Whether you want to be a CEO of a multinational company, a full-time parent, find everlasting happiness and peace in the mountains, give a TED talk, be a doctor or a teacher or even if you want to build couches, what you plan to achieve in the future contributes to your identity.

Roles and responsibilities

As time progresses, we slowly accumulate different roles and responsibilities that shape the type of person we are.

- » Child, parent, grandparent or caregiver.
- » Spouse or partner.
- » Student or teacher.
- » Friend — school friend, work friend, lifelong friend, ex-friend.
- » Employer, employee and colleague.
- » Various professional titles (e.g. owner/founder, CEO, executive, manager, supervisor, team leader, staff member, specialist/expert, intern, consultant, contractor, doctor, teacher, carpenter, tradie).
- » Player or coach.
- » Author or reader.
- » Mentor or mentee.

It's easier to appreciate how roles and responsibilities shape our identity. For example, consider how people change after becoming parents.

You might know someone who used to party every weekend but, after becoming a parent, finds joy in simpler activities like going for gentle walks, playing in the back yard, and going to bed early. Depending on the stage of life you're in, your roles and responsibilities will change and with it, so will *you*.

Relationships

The people in our life massively influence who we were, who we are, and who we will become. Perhaps one of the quickest ways to change our identity is to change the people we spend time with.

"You are the average of the 5 people
you spend the most time with."
~ Jim Rohn

» If your Dad/Mum drinks alcohol, you will probably drink too.
» If your friends smoke, you will probably smoke too.
» If you make a lot of money, you're likely have affluent friends.
» If you are really happy, the people you spend time with are likely to be happy as well.
» If you are sad, depressed and worried, you are more likely to have friends and family who are similarly struggling.

Obviously this is not a definitive rule, as there are always exceptions. Nevertheless, the concept of who you are is heavily influenced by the people you surround yourself with.

Cultural and geographical upbringing

I was born in Sri Lanka. I speak sinhalese at home. I eat with my hands. If I don't eat rice and curry for more than 12 hours, I get withdrawal symptoms. I have brown skin. I love to dance like nobody's watching. *I am Sri Lankan.*

When I was five years old, our family left Sri Lanka. Our family lived in New Zealand for five years and since then, we have lived in Australia. Australia is home. I have lived here for more than 20 years. I have an Australian accent (I am told). I got my education in Australia. I met my wife in Australia. My closest friends are wonderful people I met in Australia. Every dollar I have earnt has been in Australia. *I am Australian.*

» If I was born somewhere else, I would be different.
» If I lived somewhere else, I would be different.
» If I moved somewhere else, I would become someone different.

I am still fundamentally "me", whoever that is, but my concept of identity has evolved depending on my cultural and geographical background. For what it's worth, when the cricket is on, I am definitely still Sri Lankan.

Family upbringing

From the time we are born, to the time we leave the nest and forge our own path, we spend most of our time at home with our parents, siblings, and caregivers. These interactions, and how we interact with them, largely influence the type of person we become.

"It takes a village to raise a child."
~ African proverb

If you were born into a different household, you and your life would be different. As you get older, the concept of family evolves. Maybe you start your own family. If you have a partner or a spouse, their family may become yours. Perhaps some of your family members die or become estranged. You can't choose the family you are born into but as you get older, you can choose the family you belong to. All of these variables will influence your identity.

Education

Whether you have a PhD or didn't finish high school, your level of education contributes to your perception of identity.

When I finished medical school, I used to proudly say, "I just became a doctor." Notice the wording, *became.* There is a perceived change in core identity when we achieve a certain qualification. In my case, there is an explicit labelling of identity as it is one of the few professions where you put the qualification, "Dr", in front of your name. As you can see, identity can be artificially constructed.

Religion and spirituality

»   I *am* a Christian.

»   I *am* a Buddhist.

»   I *am* a Muslim.

»   I *am* an atheist.

»   I *am* Hindu.

»   I *am* Jewish.

Religion and spirituality, or lack of, is closely linked with who we are. For some people, it *is* who they are.

Socioeconomic status

Whether you grew up with wealth, poverty, or somewhere in between, it will affect your sense of identity.

»   I *am* rich.

»   I *am* poor.

»   I *am* middle class.

»   I *am* wealthy.

»   I *am* a millionaire.

If identity is constructed, you can appreciate that socioeconomic status is something that is prone to changing, sometimes in a given instant. For example, a millionaire could lose all of their money in a bad deal. Who are they now?

Beliefs, attitudes and values

Every "layer" of identity I have already explored will contribute to our core beliefs, attitudes, and values. These in turn, form a deep sense of identity which will affect our world views and what we determine to be important. However, these beliefs, attitudes, and values can change. For example, a parent may be strict with their children, but when they become a grandparent there seems to be an unlimited supply of chocolate and ice cream.

The five senses and our body

Our five senses allow us to see, hear, feel, smell, and taste. Without our senses, the perception of our physical body ceases to exist. Our physical body is a critical source of identity. Whether you identify as short, tall, fat, skinny, ripped, beautiful, ugly, or as Dumbo the elephant, how we perceive our physical body greatly influences our impression of who we are.

> Tracy was 43 years old and weighed 130kg. She hated being that heavy so she decided to undergo weight loss surgery.
>
> She had a gastric bypass and lost 60kg! She now weighed 70kg. This was her "dream weight". However, she was grappling with a lost sense of identity.
>
> "It's weird. I have been overweight my whole life. I am not sure who is in the mirror anymore."

Thoughts and feelings

Our inner world, the thoughts and feelings that we experience, are influenced by the circumstances of our life and how they interact with our constructed layers of identity. It is a complex and beautiful symphony that is *constantly* changing. Everything is created twice, first in our inner world and then in reality. Therefore, the workings of our inner world play a large role in determining the type of person we are. However, *Part 3* of this book, which explored the skill of psychological action, revealed our ability to control our inner world, thereby changing the concept of who we are in the process.

Looking from a different perspective

In the *Flicking the channel* chapter, I introduce the concept of *filters* that we view the world through. These are the set of prescription glasses through which we "see" the world. Our identity, and each of the layers used to construct it, are the ultimate prescription. We experience the world through the lens of each layer of our identity — the layers of "me." (See Figure 25)

We experience the world through the lens
of each layer of our identity — the layers of "me."

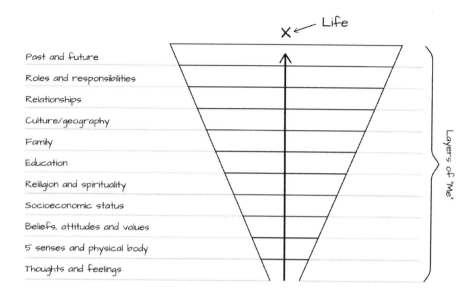

Figure 25

Let's adopt a completely different *perspective*.

If you change the vantage point so that instead of looking *outward* through the layers of "Me", you look *inward* to see what is "behind" all of these layers, what will you find? (See Figure 26)

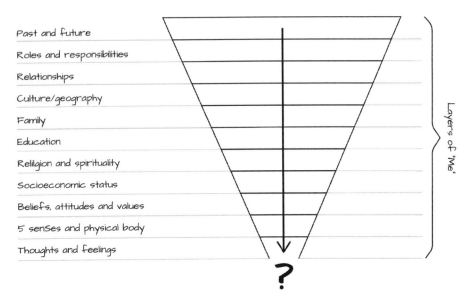

Past and future
Roles and responsibilities
Relationships
Culture/geography
Family
Education
Relilgion and spirituality
Socioeconomic status
Beliefs, attitudes and values
5 senses and physical body
Thoughts and feelings

Layers of "Me"

?

Figure 26

If you translate some of our learnings from the *Meditation for awareness* chapter, you might say that what's left is *the observer*. That would be my answer as well. If this is the case, *what or who actually is the observer?*

My honest answer is, I don't know. I may not know exactly what is left, but I can tell you one thing: *what's left is everything I will ever need.* I wish I can articulate this in words. I can't. It is beyond what words can explain. It needs to be experienced.

Perhaps you will find that beneath the layers of our constructed identity, is the real "you". There's a chance that this will lead to the realisation that "you" are already more than enough.

Perhaps you will experience that once we deconstruct each layer of our identity, we are all the *same*.

Perhaps you will contemplate not only that we are the same, but we are all *one*. Maybe this means that there is a joint stream of consciousness that connects us all.

Perhaps you will find that the world we view is much smaller than the world we view it from.

Perhaps you will find that you have the capacity for a level of happiness, joy, peace, and bliss that knows no bounds.

Perhaps this is all a load of garbage and I have completely lost the plot. At least I am happy, right?

A story from Eckhart Tolle's, *The Power of Now.*

A beggar had been sitting by the side of a road for over thirty years. One day a stranger walked by.

"Spare some change?" mumbled the beggar, mechanically holding out his old baseball cap.

"I have nothing to give you," said the stranger. Then he asked: "What's that you are sitting on?"

"Nothing," replied the beggar. "Just an old box. I have been sitting on it for as long as I can remember."

"Ever looked inside?" asked the stranger.

"No," said the beggar. "What's the point? There's nothing in there."

"Have a look inside," insisted the stranger.

The beggar managed to pry open the lid. With astonishment, disbelief, and elation, he saw that the box was filled with gold. I am that stranger who has nothing to give you and who is telling you to look inside. Not inside any box, as in the parable, but somewhere even closer: inside yourself.

Do you love who you are?

It's a big question, "Do you love who you are?"

The answer I often hear is "No," and it breaks my heart. If you don't love who you are, no matter how much you try to fill your bucket, there will always be a hole in the bottom. This whole chapter and maybe even the whole book, is dedicated to helping such people answer this question with a resounding "Yes!"

If you don't love who you are, what you may actually struggle with are certain layers of your constructed identity. This is great news because, as I hope I have demonstrated, you are *not* your constructed identity.

You are not your constructed identity.

What is powerful about looking inward and stripping away all the layers is that we are left with a profound realisation, *we are enough*. We hear this all the time, but rarely are we able to objectively verify it as the *undeniable truth*. If you take the time to strip away all the layers and look inside the "cardboard box" I hope that you can learn it for yourself.

Of course, it's not practical to strip away all the layers and stay there. We do this to gain a valuable insight: *that everything we will ever need is always accessible to us*. After that, we can put the layers back on. What's exciting is that you are now armed with the perspective that our layers of identity can change and be changed. You have the power to *decide* how to stack these layers back into your life. If there are aspects of your past that you dislike, you can learn to relate to them differently, or even let them go. If there are roles and responsibilities that don't suit you, you can change them. The layers that make up our identity can be *chosen, created,* or *let go*. This form of perspectival action grants you immense personal ownership over your happiness, your life, and the relationship you have with yourself.

Identity is constructed.
Therefore, it can be deconstructed and reconstructed.

Think of it like painting. Once all the layers are gone, you're left with an empty canvas. You may view the observer as the painter. You can choose to paint whatever you want. If you don't like something, paint over it or find somewhere else to paint. Don't worry, this particular canvas doesn't have any borders.

Letting go

We have explored how meditation can help us to *focus* and build *awareness*. The ultimate purpose of meditation is to teach us how to *let go*.

Although I can't explain in words the experience of what is left when we strip away all the layers that construct our identity, I can provide some insight into how you can potentially experience it yourself — by using meditation as a tool for letting go.

Here is the process I use for myself and the people I work with.

Letting go meditation

Find a quiet place to sit and close your eyes.

Let's go through a process of mentally letting go of each of the layers of our constructed identity. Take the time to observe the nature of your experience and reflect on what's left at each stage of letting go.

First, let go of your past and future. Imagine sitting there, with no memories of the past or plans for the future. You will notice that they still enter your mind. That's completely fine. Try you best to not "hold on" to them.

The process of letting go is like taking a tightly clenched fist and opening your hand. An open hand allows things to come and go freely. Remember, letting go is different to suppressing. We are not trying to suppress these layers of identity but rather, let go by loosening our grip on them.

Observe your current experience and contemplate what's left.

Now, let go of all of your roles and responsibilities. For example, letting go of work means that, for the purpose of this exercise, all commitments linked to this role are gone — no meetings, no clients, no boss, no timesheets, no deadlines, and no roster.

Observe your current experience and contemplate what's left.

Continue this process of letting go for each layer of your identity. Proceed to let go of your relationships, your cultural background, and where you were brought up, your family, your education, your religion and spirituality, your socioeconomic status, your beliefs, attitudes and values, your five senses, your body, and finally your thoughts and feelings.

Observe your current experience and contemplate what's left.

As you progress through this process of letting go, you will likely experience a deepening sense of happiness, peace, and joy. *Why?*

In the chapter on *Gratitude*, I introduced the analogy of the sun and the clouds. The sun is *always* there and represents our default state of happiness. The clouds are like the thoughts and feelings that obstruct the sun. To extend this further, the clouds represent the layers of our constructed identity. Once you strip away these layers, and see "behind" these clouds, you can experience the true essence of the sun itself. This essence is a state of happiness that exists beyond measure and doesn't rely on anything external. It is a form of happiness that doesn't require anything.

Everything you will ever need, you already have.
You just need to know where to look.

Dr G's prescription

The concept of identity is constructed, layer by layer. Once you learn to let go of each of these layers, you may be left with the very thing you have been searching for your whole life.

Turn to the corresponding page of your *Do Happy Workbook,* and complete the *final* exercise.

1. **Practise the letting go meditation and write down your findings.**

2. **Repeat.**

Conclusion

A Call to Action

Congratulations! You have reached the end of the book but, hopefully, this is just the beginning of a new chapter in your life.

The mental health epidemic is one of the biggest social problems we face. However, for every problem that we will ever face, someone has written a book about how to overcome it. The foundation for my happiness journey was built on reading. Books have profoundly transformed my life, and I hope that this book will do the same for you.

This book was written to provide a framework for you to better understand happiness and achieve it, *all the time*. It is an audacious task and I hope I came close. Living a full, rich, and meaningful life requires action and for us to take full personal ownership of our mental wellbeing. I hope *Do Happy* has provided you with the inspiration and the tools to do just that.

Commit to action

As you know by now, happiness is something you *do*.

Happiness =

The actions (physical, psychological, and perspectival) that contribute to a full, rich, and meaningful life.

Thank you for taking the time to read *Do Happy*.

Much love to you and of course, myself.

Dr G

Work with Dr G

If you got value out of this book, there are several ways you can work with Dr G.

Private mentoring

Dr G works with a handful of incredible and ambitious humans every year to help them become ridiculously happy, get healthier as they age, and unlock their potential so that they can achieve their biggest and most meaningful goals.

Keynote speeches and workshops

Dr G speaks on the 3 H's — Happiness, Health, and High performance. His inspiring and thought-provoking keynotes and workshops feature a unique blend of energy, humour, wit, storytelling, and sometimes dance moves.

Workplace wellbeing programs

People are the lifeblood of any organisation. If your employees are unhappy and unhealthy, they are more likely to quit, take days off, be less productive, and perform at a lower level. Dr G designs workplace wellbeing programs that equip your team with the tools they need to optimise their wellbeing and performance. When your people are happier and healthier, everything improves.

*If you are interested in working with Dr G, contact him via **drg@drgihan.com**.*

Connect with Dr G

The best way to connect with Dr G and stay updated on his work is to subscribe to his *Happiness, Health and High-Performance* newsletter. You can do this by visiting his website at www.drgihan.com or by using the QR code below. His mum thinks it's awesome and often sends him messages like, "This is a great article. I'm proud of you." She usually has good taste.

About the Author

Gihan, or 'Dr G', is a GP with a passion for lifestyle medicine. He loves to help people solve two problems: unhappiness and preventable chronic disease.

For those who are suffering with their mental health, he coaches people to take a forward looking and action-oriented approach. This helps individuals identify and achieve their goals.

For those with preventable chronic diseases such as type 2 diabetes, high blood pressure, high cholesterol, sleep apnoea, or obesity, he prefers to use lifestyle change (e.g. exercise, diet, sleep, and stress management) over prescriptions to treat, prevent, and even reverse (not a typo) conditions.

Alongside his work as a doctor, he is a mentor, speaker, and author who loves to help individuals and organisations optimise their wellbeing and performance. He writes regularly for his *Happiness, Health and High-Performance* newsletter.

Dr. Gihan Jayaweera is a dedicated medical practitioner and specialist in general practice, with years of experience in providing comprehensive health care. While deeply passionate about mental health and well-being, Dr. Gihan is not a psychologist or a specialist psychiatrist and does not hold himself out to be one. His expertise lies in general practice, where he integrates his extensive medical knowledge to support patients in achieving overall health and happiness. Dr. Gihan authored this book to share practical insights and strategies that can help individuals improve their mental well-being and lead happier lives. He encourages readers to seek personalised medical advice and support from qualified specialists for specific mental health conditions.

Acknowledgements

To my parents, I love you. This book wouldn't exist without you. Literally. Your decision to move from Sri Lanka to Australia has given me opportunities that others can only dream of. I hope I continue to make you proud with what I have chosen to do with these opportunities. You have shown me what it takes to overcome adversity. My commitment to help others is driven by the sacrifices you have made for me.

To my best friend and wife Gunya, I love you too. You have believed in me and *Do Happy* from the start. It is much easier to Do Happy with you in my life.

To Kiyan and Imaya, every decision I make is made with the two of you in mind. All I want is for you to be happy. If you are happy, everything else will fall into place. I hope this book serves as a valuable gift to the both of you as you progress in your own lives.

To my nephews and nieces, I love you all so much. You don't realise how much I think about all of you. All I want to be is a great role model for you. I hope this book provides a framework for you to follow when things get tough.

To my mother and father-in-law, I love you too. I have learnt a great deal about happiness by observing you. You model a lot of the advanced concepts in this book.

To my brother, I always look forward to our conversations. I admire your blunt form of wisdom. Thank you for teaching me that the destination is boring. Your belief that life is about being born, having a laugh, and dying is spot on. As you say, the main thing is to ensure we have a laugh.

To Erandi, you have influenced my life in ways that have completely shifted the trajectory of my life. Thank you so much for your ongoing support of me, my family, and my work.

To my 103-year-old friend "E", thank you for your sustained interest in my book. I loved when you rightfully pointed out that I had briefly "lost my hunger" for finishing it. I also love that you didn't try to help me find that hunger – you left it up to me.

To all my newsletter readers, your words of encouragement and shared excitement for this book helped me to validate my ideas and reassured me that the pages in this book were worth writing.

To my patients, your vulnerability continues to teach me the nature of the human condition. Your courage inspires me to be stronger. There would be no book without you.

To my clients, I am grateful for the trust you have placed in me to guide you on a journey towards achieving Happiness, Health, and High Performance in your life, at the same time, without compromise.

To the organisations I have worked with, thank you for allowing me to share *Do Happy* with you and your teams. It is a special privilege to impact many people at once.

To my fellow thought leaders. Thank you for inspiring me to not only write my first book, but envision writing many more.

To my work colleagues, thank you for your ongoing encouragement and buzz around the book.

To my friends, thank you for your support and care over the years. I wrote the "Relationships" chapter with all of you in mind.

To my family, thank you for loving me and wanting the best for me. The time I spend with you never feels like a waste. It is a blessing to be a part of such a beautiful group of human beings.

To Heshy P, thank you for being my spiritual "sparring partner". You are one of the most content people I know and I appreciate you sharing the simplicity of your way of life with me.

To the psychologists and health professionals who help people with their mental health every day, please know that you do such important work. I am honoured to do it alongside you.

To my mentors and coaches over the years, thank you for helping me become a better version of myself. A special mention to Dr Marli Watt who first introduced me to the NLP communication model and the concept of "neutra" circumstances which has changed the way I see life.

To Lexi, Ben and Mish from Hambone Publishing, thank you for turning my life's work into a legitimate book.

To the authors that take the time to download years of their learnings into a single book, my deepest gratitude goes out to you. For every problem we face, someone has written a book about it. I know this to be true because the books that I have read and continue to read have solved many problems in my life.

References

Introduction

1. Australian Bureau of Statistics (ABS): https://www.abs.gov.au/statistics/health/mental-health
   Australian Institute of Health and Welfare (AIHW): https://www.aihw.gov.au/mental-health

2. https://www.abs.gov.au/statistics/health/mental-health/national-study-mental-health-and-wellbeing/2020-2022

3. https://www.aihw.gov.au/mental-health/overview/prevalence-and-impact-of-mental-illness

4. Donne, John. The Works of John Donne. vol III, Henry Alford, ed. London: John W. Parker, 1839. 574-5.

Part 2 — Fundamental Skills — Physical Action

5. Singh, Ben et al. "Effectiveness of physical activity interventions for improving depression, anxiety and distress: an overview of systematic reviews." *British Journal Of Sports Medicine* vol. 57,18 (2023)

6.   Mammen, George and Guy Faulkner. "Physical Activity and the Prevention of Depression: A systematic review of prospective studies." *American Journal of Preventative Medicine* vol. 45, 5 (2013)

7.   Richards, Justin et al. "Don't worry, be happy: cross-sectional associations between physical activity and happiness in 15 European countries." *BMC public health* vol. 15 53. 31 Jan. 2015

8.   Lathia, Neal et al. "Happier People Live More Active Lives: Using Smartphones to Link Happiness and Physical Activity." *PloS one* vol. 12,1 e0160589. 4 Jan. 2017

9.   *Foundations of Lifestyle Medicine Board Review Manual*, ASLM

10. Australian Bureau of Statistics (ABS): https://www.abs.gov.au/statistics/health/health-conditions-and-risks/physical-activity/latest-release

11. Australian Government, Department of Health and Aged Care: https://www.health.gov.au/topics/physical-activity-and-exercise/physical-activity-and-exercise-guidelines-for-all-australians/for-adults-18-to-64-years

12. Scott, A. J., Webb, T. L., Martyn-St James, M., Rowse, G., & Weich, S. (2021). Improving sleep quality leads to better mental health: A meta-analysis of randomised controlled trials. *Sleep medicine reviews, 60,* 101556. https://doi.org/10.1016/j.smrv.2021.101556

13. Gardiner, Carissa et al. "The effect of caffeine on subsequent sleep: A systematic review and meta-analysis." Sleep medicine reviews vol. 69 (2023)

14. American Psychological Association, Stress and Sleep: https://www.apa.org/news/press/releases/stress/2013/sleep

15. Australian Institute of Health and Welfare. Sleep problems as a risk factor for chronic conditions. AIHW, 2021.

16. Dr. Matt Walker, The Biology of Sleep and Your Unique Sleep Needs, https://youtu.be/-OBCwiPPfEU?si=mKKqvlWMQY_w2bOy

17. Australian Sleep Association, Chronic Insomnia: https://www.sleepprimarycareresources.org.au/insomnia/basic-sleep-and-sleep-hygiene-education?q=stages%20of%20sleep

18. Deakin University, Food & Mood Centre: https://foodandmoodcentre.com.au/resources/

19. Sender, Ron et al. "Revised Estimates for the Number of Human and Bacteria Cells in the Body." PLoS biology vol. 14,8 e1002533. 19 Aug. 2016

20. Abbott, A. Scientists bust myth that our bodies have more bacteria than human cells. Nature (2016).

21. Dash, Sarah et al. "The gut microbiome and diet in psychiatry: focus on depression." Current opinion in psychiatry vol. 28,1 (2015): 1-6.

22. Appleton, Jeremy. "The Gut-Brain Axis: Influence of Microbiota on Mood and Mental Health." *Integrative medicine (Encinitas, Calif.)* vol. 17,4 (2018): 28-32.

23. Food and Mood Centre, https://foodandmoodcentre.com.au/wp-content/uploads/sites/129/2022/12/Food-and-Mood-MH-Consumer-Guides.pdf

24. Australian Institute of Health and Welfare. (2024). *Alcohol, tobacco & other drugs in Australia*

25. Health Direct, Drinking water and your health https://www.healthdirect.gov.au/drinking-water-and-your-health

26. Australian Government, Department of Health and Aged Care, "What is alcohol?" https://www.health.gov.au/topics/alcohol/about-alcohol/what-is-alcohol

27. Australian Bureau of Statistics. (2022). *Waist circumference and BMI.* ABS. https://www.abs.gov.au/statistics/health/health-conditions-and-risks/waist-circumference-and-bmi/latest-release.

28. Jung, Franziska U C E et al. "The relationship between weight history and psychological health-Differences related to gender and weight loss patterns." *PloS one* vol. 18,2 e0281776. 13 Feb. 2023

29. Chen, Yijing et al. "Regulation of Neurotransmitters by the Gut Microbiota and Effects on Cognition in Neurological Disorders." *Nutrients* vol. 13,6 2099. 19 Jun. 2021

30. Appleton, Jeremy. "The Gut-Brain Axis: Influence of Microbiota on Mood and Mental Health." *Integrative medicine (Encinitas, Calif.)* vol. 17,4 (2018): 28-32.

31. Food and Mood Centre, "Clinical Practice Guidelines" https://foodandmoodcentre.com.au/wp-content/uploads/sites/129/2022/10/MH-Clinical-Practice-Guidelines-MH-Consumer-Guides-UpdatedAug2022.pdf

32. TED. Robert Waldinger: What makes a good life? Lessons from the longest study on happiness. https://www.youtube.com/watch?v=8KkKuTCFvzI

33. Richard Louv, "What is Nature-Deficit Disorder?" https://richardlouv.com/blog/what-is-nature-deficit-disorder

34. Tomasso, Linda Powers et al. "The Relationship between Nature Deprivation and Individual Wellbeing across Urban Gradients under COVID-19." *International journal of environmental research and public health* vol. 18,4 1511. 5 Feb. 2021

35. Jimenez, Marcia P et al. "Associations between Nature Exposure and Health: A Review of the Evidence." *International journal of environmental research and public health* vol. 18,9 4790. 30 Apr. 2021

36. Fogg, Brian J. 2019. *Tiny Habits : The Small Changes That Change Everything.* London: Virgin Books.

37. Fryburg, David A. "Kindness as a Stress Reduction-Health Promotion Intervention: A Review of the Psychobiology of Caring." *American journal of lifestyle medicine* vol. 16,1 89-100. 29 Jan. 2021

38. Moche, H., & Västfjäll, D. (2021). To give or to take money? The effects of choice on prosocial spending and happiness. *The Journal of Positive Psychology, 17*(5), 742–753.

39. The Greater Good Science Center, "The Science of Generosity" https://ggsc.berkeley.edu/images/uploads/GGSC-JTF_White_Paper-Generosity-FINAL.pdf

40. Emmons, R. A., & McCullough, M. E. (2003). "Counting blessings versus burdens: An experimental investigation of gratitude and subjective well-being in daily life." Greater Good Science Center. https://greatergood.berkeley.edu/pdfs/GratitudePDFs/6Emmons-BlessingsBurdens.pdf

41. Shapiro, S. L. (2015, November 3). "How gratitude leads to a happier life." *Psychology Today.* https://www.psychologytoday.com/au/blog/the-mindful-self-express/201511/how-gratitude-leads-to-a-happier-life

42. Fredrickson, B L. "The role of positive emotions in positive psychology. The broaden-and-build theory of positive emotions." *The American psychologist* vol. 56,3 (2001)

43. Sample, I. (2010, November 11). Wandering mind not a happy mind. *Harvard Gazette*. https://news.harvard.edu/gazette/story/2010/11/wandering-mind-not-a-happy-mind/

44. Shakya, H. B., & Christakis, N. A. (2017, April 10). A new, more rigorous study confirms: The more you use Facebook, the worse you feel. *Harvard Business Review*. https://hbr.org/2017/04/a-new-more-rigorous-study-confirms-the-more-you-use-facebook-the-worse-you-feel

45. Shakya, Holly B, and Nicholas A Christakis. "Association of Facebook Use With Compromised Well-Being: A Longitudinal Study." *American journal of epidemiology* vol. 185,3 (2017): 203-211.

46. Feinstein, B. A., Hershenberg, R., Bhatia, V., Latack, J. A., Meuwly, N., & Davila, J. (2013). Negative social comparison on Facebook and depressive symptoms: Rumination as a mechanism. *Psychology of Popular Media Culture, 2*(3), 161–170.

47. Helmut Appel, Alexander L Gerlach, Jan Crusius. "The interplay between Facebook use, social comparison, envy, and depression" *Current Opinion in Psychology* vol. 9 (2016): 44-49

48. Nakshine, Vaishnavi S et al. "Increased Screen Time as a Cause of Declining Physical, Psychological Health, and Sleep Patterns: A Literary Review." *Cureus* vol. 14,10 e30051. 8 Oct. 2022

49. Brewer, Judson, and Jon Kabat-Zinn. 2017. *The Craving Mind: From Cigarettes to Smartphones to Love — Why We Get Hooked and How We Can Break Bad Habits*. New Haven: Yale University Press.

50. Transport Accident Commission. *The facts: Distractions and driving.* https://www.tac.vic.gov.au/road-safety/staying-safe/distracted-driving/the-facts-distractions-and-driving

51. https://pubmed.ncbi.nlm.nih.gov/36796860/
www.ncbi.nlm.nih.gov/pmc/articles/PMC6146362/
www.sciencedirect.com/science/article/abs/pii/S0749379713004510
www.ncbi.nlm.nih.gov/pmc/articles/PMC4320474/
www.ncbi.nlm.nih.gov/pmc/articles/PMC5213770/
ASLM book Foundations of Lifestyle Medicine Board Review
Manual

52. https://www.abs.gov.au/statistics/health/health-conditions-and-risks/
physical-activity/latest-release

53. https://www.health.gov.au/topics/physical-activity-and-exercise/
physical-activity-and-exercise-guidelines-for-all-australians/for-adults-
18-to-64-years

54. Ong, Jason C. 2017. *Mindfulness-Based Therapy for Insomnia.*
Washington, Dc: American Psychological Association.

55. https://pubmed.ncbi.nlm.nih.gov/36870101/
https://www.ncbi.nlm.nih.gov/pmc/articles/PMC6292246/

56. https://www.apa.org/news/press/releases/stress/2013/sleep

57. https://www.aihw.gov.au/reports/risk-factors/sleep-problems-as-a-risk-
factor/summary

58. https://www.youtube.com/watch?v=-OBCwiPPfEU&ab_
channel=AndrewHuberman

59. https://www.sleepprimarycareresources.org.au/insomnia/basic-sleep-
and-sleep-hygiene-education?q=stages%20of%20sleep

60. https://www.sleepprimarycareresources.org.au/insomnia/basic-sleep-
and-sleep-hygiene-education?q=stages%20of%20sleep

61. https://www.sleepprimarycareresources.org.au/insomnia/basic-sleep-
and-sleep-hygiene-education?q=stages%20of%20sleep

62. https://www.sleepprimarycareresources.org.au/insomnia/basic-sleep-and-sleep-hygiene-education?q=stages%20of%20sleep

63. https://foodandmoodcentre.com.au/resources/

64. https://www.nature.com/articles/nature.2016.19136#:~:text=It%27s%20often%20said%20that%20the,to%2Done%2C%20they%20calculate.

65. https://pubmed.ncbi.nlm.nih.gov/25415497/
https://www.health.qld.gov.au/newsroom/features/the-links-between-your-gut-microbiome-and-mental-health-is-your-bug-half-affecting-your-mental-wellbeing

66. https://www.ncbi.nlm.nih.gov/pmc/articles/PMC6469458/
https://foodandmoodcentre.com.au/wp-content/uploads/sites/129/2022/10/MH-Clinical-Practice-Guidelines-MH-Consumer-Guides-UpdatedAug2022.pdf

67. Pollan, Michael. 2009. *Food Rules : An Eater's Manual*. New York, N.Y. Penguin Books.

68. https://foodandmoodcentre.com.au/wp-content/uploads/sites/129/2022/12/Food-and-Mood-MH-Consumer-Guides.pdf

69. https://www.youtube.com/watch?v=-OBCwiPPfEU&ab_channel=AndrewHuberman

70. https://www.tac.vic.gov.au/road-safety/staying-safe/distracted-driving/the-facts-distractions-and-driving

Part 3 —Intermediate Skills — Psychological Action

71. Sagiv, L., Roccas, S., Cieciuch, J. *et al.* Personal values in human life. *Nature Human Behaviour* 1, 630–639 (2017).

72. Happonen, S. (n.d.). *Core values list*. Saturday Gift. https://www.saturdaygift.com/core-values-list/

73. Dr Russ Harris. 2013. *Happiness Trap, The: Stop Struggling, Start Living.* Exisle Publishing.

74. Rosen, C. (2023, August 16). Why being poor may be associated with higher life satisfaction. *Big Think.* https://bigthink.com/the-present/poor-with-high-life-satisfaction/

75. Kaplan, J. (2022, April 12). Heiress Abigail Disney says "billionaires are miserable, unhappy people," and it's time for change: "The billionaire bashing needs to happen. I don't know why we're being so polite." *Business Insider.* https://www.businessinsider.com/abigail-disney-patriotic-millionaires-billionaires-miserable-unhappy-people-wealth-tax-2022-4

76. Galbraith, E.D., et al. (2024, February 5). "High life satisfaction reported among small-scale societies with low incomes." *PNAS.* Vol. 121 No.7. https://www.pnas.org/doi/abs/10.1073/pnas.2311703121

77. Holfter, Gisela. 2011. *Heinrich Böll and Ireland.* Cambridge Scholars Publishing.

78. Eckhart Tolle. 2018. *The Power of Now : A Guide to Spiritual Enlightenment.* Sydney, Nsw: Hachette Australia.

Part 4: The Advanced Skills — Perspectival action

79. Brahm, Ajahn. 2010. *Opening the Door of Your Heart.* Hachette UK.

80. Buddhist Society of Western Australia, https://bswa.org/

Made in the USA
Middletown, DE
18 March 2025

72926172R00234